WARS OF EMPIRE

WARS OF EMPIRE

DOUGLAS PORCH

Series Editor, John Keegan

 Smithsonian Books

Collins

An Imprint of HarperCollins*Publishers*

Published in 2006 in the United States of America by Smithsonian Books
In association with Cassell
Wellington House, 125 Strand
London, WC2R 0BB

Library of Congress Cataloging-in-Publication Data has been applied for.
ISBN-10: 0-06-085142-2
ISBN-13: 978-0-06-085142-2

Manufactured in Spain, not at government expense.

Cartography: Arcadia Editions, Ltd.
Designer: Richard Carr
Picture research: Elaine Willis
Printed and bound in Spain

Title Page: *British troops lift the siege of Lucknow, 19 March 1858. The Indian
Mutiny (1857–8) ended the reign of the East India Company and its private army
and significantly altered British policies toward the recruitment and arming of their
imperial forces in India.*

Overleaf: *A 4.7" naval gun fires at Boer trenches at Magersfontein in December 1899.*

Acknowledgements

This is a book about an aspect of warfare that is often regarded as a secondary, even irrelevant, to the general development of conflict in the modern era. Contemporary, technologically sophisticated armies pitted against primitive opponents offered little more than a recipe for a slow march to an inevitable conclusion. This judgement requires re-evaluation. First, for an allegedly minor mode of warfare, imperial conflict proved a persistent feature of military activity from the mid eighteenth century to the First World War and beyond. Wars of empire helped to make Wolfe and Montcalm, Clive and Dupleix, Wellington and Tipu Sultan, Gordon and Kitchener, Custer and Sitting Bull, Gallieni and Lyautey household names. Furthermore, the imperial general was also a proconsul, forced to rely on his political skills as much as his operational expertise to prevail. War, Clausewitz reminds us, is politics, and nowhere was this more accurate than in the imperial arena. Imperial warfare determined winners and losers among developed nations in the struggle for world standing and in the fulfilment of national aspirations. It also sealed the fate of indigenous regimes and determined the destiny of great stretches of the globe. Finally, the end of the Cold War has witnessed an explosion of peacekeeping operations, a lineal descendant of wars of empire. Imperialism was never popular in its own day. Every good imperial commander knew that he must deliver military success at low cost. History is not about supplying 'lessons' for the future. It tells its own story. But no modern commander in Kosovo or East Timor can ignore the perils of conducting operations, far from home, with a narrow political base of support, any more than could his predecessors in earlier centuries in Africa or Asia.

I would like to thank John Keegan for offering me the opportunity to write this volume, and Penny Gardiner for shepherding it through to publication. Finally, I am deeply indebted to my agent, Gill Coleridge, for her support, encouragement and enthusiasm over the years.

DOUGLAS PORCH
Monterey

Contents

KEY TO MAPS

Military units–size

XXXXX ☐	army group
XXXX ☐	army
XXX ☐	corps
XX ☐	division
X ☐	brigade
III ☐	regiment
II ☐	battalion

Military movements

➤	attack
⇢	retreat
✈	air attack
✕	battle
▩	fortress

Geographical symbols

▬	urban area
——	road
▭▬▭	railway
——	river
- - -	seasonal river
⊥⊥⊥	canal
——	border
⊃⊂	bridge or pass

Map list

Chronology

1742	Beginning of War of Austrian Succession.
1744	King George's War.
1745	Louisbourg captured.
1746	Choctaw Revolt; French fleet fails to retake Louisbourg; Dupleix seizes Madras.
1747	Bostonians rebel at British attempts to impress sailors.
1748	Treaty of Aix-la-Chapelle ends War of Austrian Succession; Louisbourg returned to France; first British commander-in-chief appointed for India.
1749	Halifax established in Nova Scotia to mask Louisbourg and intimidate the Acadians; English traders appear in the Ohio valley; French expedition under Céleron de Blainville attempts to establish French sovereignty in the Ohio valley.
1753	Duquesne builds three forts on Allegheny river; Amerindians ask Virginia colonists for help in expelling them.
1754	Expedition to Ohio Forks under Washington ambushed a French force and subsequently surrendered to a larger French force at Fort Necessity; British dispatched reinforcements to America under Edward Braddock; first royal regiment sent to India; Dupleix recalled to France.
1755	French reinforced Quebec with forces under Baron Dieskau; Braddock's force ambushed on way to Fort Duquesne; Dieskau wounded at the battle of Lake George and abandoned by his Mohawk allies.
1756	British reinforce American garrisons; Montcalm besieges Oswego; Black Hole of Calcutta incident (20 June).
1757	'Massacre' of Fort William Henry garrison; Clive defeats an Indian–French force at Plassey in Bengal.
1758	British seize Louisbourg and Fort Duquesne (Pittsburg); fail to take Fort Carillon (Ticonderoga).
1759	Fall of Quebec to Wolfe; French abandon Forts Carillon and St Frédéric; battle of Quiberon Bay in November cripples French fleet and prevents reinforcements; British capture Guadeloupe; French abandon siege of Madras.

1760   Battle of Sainte-Foy (28 April) ends French attempt to retake Quebec; Montreal and French Canada falls to Amherst; Eyre Coote drives French back to Pondicherry.

1761   British forces continue to seize French possessions in India, the West Indies and West Africa.

1762   Capture of Havana, Martinique, St Lucia, Grenada and St Vincent by the British; British expedition sailed from Madras to capture Manila.

1763   Treaty of Paris ends Seven Years War. Britain returns French West Indies in exchange for Canada; Havana restored to Spain in return for Florida.

1764   Mutiny of East India Company's Bengal army is crushed.

1765   Declaratory Act affirms Britain's right to tax American colonies; northern Circars and Madras ceded to East India Company.

1766   Robert Clive leaves India; First Mysore War (1766–9); Louis de Bougainville begins voyage to the Pacific that will result in the discoveries of Tahiti, the Solomon Islands and New Guinea.

1768   Secretary of State for Colonies appointed in Britain; Gurkhas conquer Nepal; Cook sets out on his first voyage of circumnavigation (1768–71).

1769   Privy Council in London affirms retention of tea duty in American colonies.

1770   'Boston Massacre'; Cook discovers Australia.

1772   James Bruce reaches confluence of Blue and White Niles; Captain Cook leaves England on second voyage of circumnavigation (1772–5).

1773   East India Company Regulating Act; Boston Tea Party.

1774   Coercive Acts passed against Massachusetts; Continental Congress meets in Philadelphia.

1775   American Revolution begins; British defeat at Lexington followed by costly victory at Bunker Hill outside Boston; Second Continental Congress assembles at Philadelphia; American attack on Quebec fails.

1776   Declaration of Independence; Washington escapes destruction at battle of Long Island; Washington defeats British at Trenton on Christmas Eve; Cook's third voyage to the Pacific begins; Adam Smith publishes *Wealth of Nations* which condemns mercantile theory of colonial economics.

1777   Lafayette arrives in America; Washington drives British out of New Jersey; British defeat Washington at Brandywine and seize Philadelphia; Burgoyne capitulates at Saratoga; Washington retires to Valley Forge, Pa.

1778   American colonies sign treaties with France and Holland, reject British offer of peace; British evacuate Philadelphia for New York; French troops under Rochambeau arrive in Newport, RI; Warren Hastings captures Chandernagore in Bengal; Cook discovers Hawaii.

1779   Spain declares war on Britain and lays siege to Gibraltar (1779–83); British campaign against the Maratha (1779–82) begins in India; Cook murdered in Hawaii.

1780   Military stalemate in American Revolutionary War; Charleston, SC, falls to the British; Cornwallis defeats Americans at Camden; Second Mysore War (1780–84).

1781   Greene leads British on an exhausting chase through South Carolina, North Carolina and Virginia; British capitulation at Yorktown, and evacuation of Charleston and Savannah effectively ends war of the American Revolution.

1782   Peace talks open between Britain and the American revolutionaries; Spain captures Minorca from the British; Maratha War ends; Tipu Sultan becomes sultan of Mysore; Admiral Howe relieves Gibraltar; Spain completes conquest of Florida; Rodney wins battle of the Saintes assuring British naval supremacy in American waters.

1783   Peace of Versailles ends War of the American Revolution.

1784   William Pitt the Younger's India Act substantially increases the government's control over the East India Company.

1785   Warren Hastings resigns as Governor General of India.

1786   Cornwallis made Governor-General of India.

1789   Outbreak of French Revolution; Tipu Sultan invades Travancore.

1790   Third Mysore War (1790–92)

1791   Toussaint l'Ouverture joins insurgency against French in Saint Domingue.

1792   Thomas Paine publishes *Rights of Man*; Tipu Sultan defeated by Cornwallis.

1795	Dutch surrender Ceylon to the British; British occupy Cape of Good Hope; Mungo Park explores the Niger river.
1796	Chinese authorities forbid the importation of opium; East India Company's forces reorganized.
1797	Lord Richard Wellesley (1760–1842), brother of the future duke, appointed Governor-General of India; Naval battle of St Vincent; Toussaint l'Ouverture consolidates rule over Saint Domingue.
1798	Treaty of Hyderabad signed between Britain and the Nizam; Napoleon captures Egypt.
1799	Tipu Sultan killed at Seringapatam; Arthur Wellesley (the future Duke) named governor of Mysore.
1800	British capture Malta; defeat French at Aboukir.
1801	Department of War and Colonies made responsible for colonial policy.
1802	West India docks built in London; French expedition arrives in Saint Domingue.
1803	Henry Shrapnel (1761–1842) invents the fragmentation shell; Arthur Wellesley defeats Marathas at battle of Assaye; death of Toussaint l'Ouverture.
1804	War between British and Holkar of Indore.
1805	Modern Egypt established with Mehemet Ali as Pasha; Wellesley departs India; Battle of Trafalgar.
1806	First English invasion of Buenos Aires.
1807	Second English invasion of Buenos Aires; slave trade to British colonies prohibited; United States bans importation of slaves.
1808	Napoleonic invasion of Spain; source of Ganges discovered.
1809	British capture Martinique and Cayenne from French; Revolutions in La Paz and Quinto.
1810	British capture Guadaloupe; Revolutions in Buenos Aires and Bogotá. Second revolution in Quinto; Simon Bolívar emerges as 'The Liberator'.
1811	British occupy Java; Paraguay and Venezuela declare independence.
1812	Spanish royalists retake Quinto.
1813	East India Company's monopoly abolished; Bolívar proclaims war to the death against Spain; Russia seizes Dagestan.
1814	Ferdinand VII regains throne in Spain.

1815   Argentine army takes Potosí.

1816   Britain restores Java to the Netherlands; British bombard Algiers; Argentine provinces declare independence.

1817   San Martín crosses Andes into Chile; defeats Spanish at Chacubuco.

1818   End of Maratha Wars; Rajput States and Poona come under British rule; Martín defeats Spanish at Maipó; Chile declares independence; border between Canada and the United States agreed upon at the forty-ninth parallel.

1819   East India Company establishes settlement at Singapore; Bolívar establishes greater Colombia.

1820   Spanish troops en route to colonies rebel in Cadiz.

1821   San Martín declares Peruvian independence; Venezuelan independence confirmed by Bolívar's defeat of Spanish forces at the battle of Carabobo; Guatemala, Mexico, Panama and Santo Domingo achieve independence from Spain.

1822   Bolívar and San Martín meet at Guayaquil; Ecuador, Colombia and Venezuela form a single state; Brazil achieves independence from Portugal.

1823   Monroe Doctrine effectively prevents new colonial settlements in the Western hemisphere by European imperial powers.

1824   First Burmese War (1824–6); British capture Rangoon; battle of Ayacucho (9 December) ends wars of South American independence.

1825   Bolivia declares independence.

1827   Dey of Algiers hits French consul with a fly whisk.

1829   Suttee (burning of Hindu widows) abolished in Bengal.

1830   Mysore added to British possessions in India; French invade Algiers to avenge insult to consul.

1831   Darwin begins his voyage on *The Beagle*.

1832   Britain occupies Falkland Islands; Abd el-Kader becomes emir of Mascara.

1833   Abolition of slavery throughout British Empire.

1834   Mehemet Ali founds a dynasty in Egypt that will last until 1952; Shamil elected imam of Dagestan.

1835   French defeated by Abd el-Kader at Macta Marshes; Second Seminole War begins (1835–42).

1836   'The Great Trek' begins north from Cape; Bugeaud defeats Abd el-Kader at Sikkak river.

1837   Revolts in Upper and Lower Canada; Osceola seized under a flag of truce.

1838   Afrikaners defeat the Zulus at the battle of Blood river in Natal; First British–Afghan War (1838–42); first steamships cross Atlantic from Britain to the United States; Russians take Shamil's capital at Ahuglo.

1839   First Opium War (1839–42); Afrikaner trekkers found republic of Natal; British invade Afghanistan.

1840   Lower and Upper Canada united; Abd el-Kader attacks French settlers on Mitidja Plain.

1841   British proclaim sovereignty over Hong Kong; New Zealand recognized as a British colony; Napier arrives in Sind; Bugeaud returns to Algiers.

1842   Treaty of Nanking ends Opium War; Afrikaner trekkers establish Orange Free State; British began withdrawal from Kabul.

1843   Natal annexed by Britain; Sind campaign ends in conquest and annexation; Maori revolts in New Zealand.

1844   Southern Maratha campaign; Bugeaud defeats Abd el-Kader at Isly.

1845   First British–Sikh War begins; further Maori uprisings in New Zealand.

1846   Treaty of Lahore ends First Sikh War; Seventh Kaffir War (1846–7) begins in South Africa.

1847   Bugeaud resigns as governor general of Algeria; Abd el-Kader surrenders to French.

1848   Second British–Sikh War; France abolishes slavery in West Indies.

1849   British annex Punjab.

1850   Taiping rebellion in China.

1851   Beginning of Burma War.

1852   The South African Republic (the Transvaal) established; Second Burmese War (1852–3).

1853   East India Company annexes Nagpur.

1854   Outbreak of Crimean War (1854–6); Ferdinand de Lesseps granted concession by Egypt to construct the Suez Canal; Faidherbe named Governor-General of Senegal.

1855	Taiping rebellion ends.
1856	British East India Company annexes Oudh; Natal established as a Crown colony.
1857	Indian Mutiny (1857–8); British destroy Chinese fleet.
1858	East India Company forces transferred to the British Crown; campaigns on north-west frontier of India; Treaty of Tientsin ends Anglo-Chinese War; Suez Company formed.
1859	Work on Suez Canal begins; Shamil surrenders to Russians.
1860	Second Maori War (1860–70); Anglo-French forces defeat Chinese at Pa-li Chau. Treaty of Peking signed; amalgamation of the Indian Army; reorganization of Bengal, Madras and Bombay armies.
1861	Sikkim campaign.
1862	R. J. Gatling (1818–1903) constructs the gun that bears his name; French troops invade Mexico.
1863	Battle of Camerone in Mexico.
1864	French take Cochin-China (Vietnam).
1865	War between Orange Free State and the Basuto (1865–6).
1866	Fenian raids in Canada; British campaign against Indians of British Honduras.
1867	British North America Act establishes dominion of Canada; diamonds discovered in South Africa; French depart Mexico.
1868	British forces invade Abyssinia; campaigns on north-west frontier of India.
1869	Red river Rebellion in Canada; opening of the Suez Canal.
1870	British force under Wolseley ends Red River Rebellion; Franco-Prussian War (1870–71).
1871	Britain annexes diamond fields of Kimberley.
1872	Cape Colony granted self-government.
1873	Ashanti War (1873–4).
1874	Disraeli becomes Prime Minister.
1875	British government buys khedive of Egypt's shares in the Suez Canal Company.
1876	Victoria proclaimed Empress of India; Custer annihilated at the Little Bighorn (25 June).
1877	British annexation of Transvaal.
1878	Second Afghan War (1878–80).

1879   Zulu Wars end in British victory after humiliating defeat at
       Isandlwana; Britain deposes Ismail, khedive of Egypt.
1880   Transvaal declares itself independent of Britain, igniting First
       South African (Boer) War; Roberts defeats Ayub Khan near
       Qandahar (1 September).
1881   Transvaal rebels defeat British at Majuba Hill; Britain recognizes
       Transvaal independence; French occupy Tunis; French offensive
       against Samori.
1882   British invade Egypt; occupy Cairo and canal zone.
1883   British decide to evacuate Sudan in face of nationalist uprising
       led by the Mahdi; Paul Kruger becomes President of the South
       African Republic (the Transvaal); French invade Annam and
       Tonkin.
1884   General Gordon reaches Khartoum; Germany occupies South-
       West Africa; Berlin Congress decides on 'effective occupation' as
       prerequisite to colonial claims.
1885   Death of Gordon at Khartoum; British and Egyptian forces
       evacuate the Sudan; invasion of Upper Burma; suppression of
       Riel's rebellion in north-west Canada; Germany annexes
       Tanganyika and Zanzibar; the Congo becomes the personal
       possession of King Leopold of the Belgians; abortive French
       attempt to take Madagascar; French setback at Lang Son (Tonkin)
       results in overthrow of the Ferry government.
1886   First meeting of Indian National Congress; Burma incorporated in
       Indian Empire; capture of Geronimo.
1887   First Colonial Conference opens in London; British East Africa
       Company chartered.
1888   Sikkim War; Matabele accept British protection and grant Cecil
       Rhodes mining rights; Sarawak becomes a British protectorate;
       rebellion against Samori in part of his empire.
1889   Ghost Dance movement revived among Amerindians during solar
       eclipse in January.
1890   Britain exchanges Heligoland with Germany for Zanzibar and
       Pemba; Cecil Rhodes becomes Prime Minister of Cape Colony;
       publication of Alfred Thayer Mahan's *The Influence of Sea Power
       upon History*; battle of Wounded Knee (South Dakota)
       (29 December) ends Ghost Dance movement among Sioux.

1891	Pan-German League founded; French offensive against Samori.
1892	Gladstone becomes Prime Minister; French invade Dahomey.
1893	Matebele expedition.
1894	British South Africa Company completes occupation of Matabeleland; Uganda becomes a British protectorate; Gambia expedition; Bonnier massacred after reaching Timbuktu.
1895	Abolition of separate armies in India; territory south of Zambezi renamed Rhodesia; French invade Madagascar.
1896	Jameson Raid crushed; Kaiser sends 'Kruger telegram' in support of Transvaal; Rhodes resigns as premier of Cape; Transvaal and Orange Free State form a military alliance; Italian forces defeated by Abyssinians at Adowa; Kitchener begins reconquest of the Sudan; Matabele revolt suppressed; Federated Malay States formed; Bechuanaland expedition; first edition of C. E. Callwell's *Small Wars*; Marchand mission sets out from the mouth of the Congo river.
1897	Colonial Conference in London.
1898	Kruger re-elected president of the Transvaal; Britain obtains ninety-nine-year lease on Kowloon and New Territories adjacent to Hong Kong; Kitchener wins Omdurman and sails to Fashoda to confront Marchand; Boxer uprising in China against foreign interference; United States declares war on Spain, occupies Cuba, Guam, Puerto Rico and the Philippines; Samori captured by the French; Voulet–Chanoine Mission (1898–9).
1899	Anglo-Egyptian Sudan Convention; Sudan becomes a condominium; outbreak of Boer War witnesses British defeats of 'Black Week'; Roberts becomes commander-in-chief in December with Kitchener as Chief of Staff; Aguinaldo elected president of the Philippine Republic (23 January).
1900	Relief of Mafeking and Ladysmith, annexation of the Orange Free State and the Transvaal; beginning of guerrilla war; Kitchener becomes commander-in-chief in December; Lamy killed in the conquest of Lake Chad; Boxer Rebellion.
1901	Guerrilla warfare intensifies in South Africa; Aguinaldo captured (23 March) in Luzon.

1902	Boer War ends. J. A. Hobson publishes *Imperialism*; battle of Tit assures French control of Tuareg of the Algerian Sahara.
1903	Reorganization of British forces into a single Indian Army; Britain completed conquest of northern Nigeria; Lyautey reports as commander of Sud-Oranais on Moroccan–Algerian border.
1904	Anglo-French entente exchanges free hand for French in Morocco against dropping French claims in Egypt; Russo-Japanese War (1904–5); Marchand resigns from the French Army.
1905	Louis Botha demands responsible self-government for Transvaal; Kaiser recognizes Moroccan independence at Tangier in an attempt to split Anglo-French *entente*; Port Arthur surrenders (2 January), battle of Tsushima Strait (27 May).
1906	British force Turkey to cede the Sinai to Egypt; Britain and China agree to a reduction in opium production; Algeciras conference over future of Morocco.
1907	Britain and France agree to guarantee Siamese independence.
1908	French and Spanish troops occupy Casablanca after riots against Europeans there; Anglo-Russian *entente*.
1909	Act for the Union of South Africa passed by British Parliament; Indian Councils Act extends the franchise.
1910	Union of South Africa achieved; Charles Mangin publishes *La force noire*.
1911	Delhi durbar of the King-Emperor George V; Agadir crisis precipitated by French occupation of Fez.
1912	French begin to occupy much of Morocco; Mangin captures Marrakesh.
1913	Balkan Wars; fighting continues in Morocco.
1914	Outbreak of First World War.

From Trade
to Conquest

*Dom Henrique, alias Prince Henry the Navigator
(1394–1460), the impresario of the 'Age of
Discovery'. His base at Sagres became a centre
where geographers, map makers, ship designers,
explorers and venture capitalists plotted the
circumvention of the Islamic world. Papal Bulls
sanctioned the masterful attitude adopted by the
Portuguese, and subsequently all Europeans,
towards races beyond the pale of Christendom.*

From Trade to Conquest

I N THE IMMEDIATE aftermath of Soviet Communism's collapse, victorious 'Cold Warriors' expressed the optimistic view that a new world order based on the triumph of Western values would replace the ideological frontiers which had earlier divided the world. Not everyone agreed. The American political scientist, Samuel Huntington, led a chorus of academics and journalists who put forward a counter-opinion, that the abolition of the ideological divisions of the Cold War would unleash tensions and animosities repressed during the half century of Soviet–Western conflict. Any 'new world order', Huntington argued, would be likely to resemble a previous world's disorder, a relapse into chaos anchored in antique animosities swathed in the certainties of religion, custom and tradition. In fact, what Huntington and others have suggested is that the end of the Cold War has resurrected a situation similar to that faced by nineteenth-century imperialists. These were people who believed that the expansion of trade, Christianity and the scientific knowledge and administrative skills of the West would expand the boundaries of civilization and reduce zones of conflict. Through imperialism, poverty would be transformed into prosperity, the savage would be saved, superstition would vanish into enlightenment, and order would be imposed where once only turmoil and barbarism reigned.

Imperialism provoked a clash of civilizations not unlike that observed by Huntington in today's international system. As in the modern era, there were places in the eighteenth and nineteenth centuries where chaos was not in Western interests. It disrupted trade patterns or threatened the 'oil spots' of Western settlement. The barbarism of foreign beliefs, customs and practices sometimes offended the West's humanitarian instincts. As today, crisis resolution then often required armed intervention. The peace operations and humanitarian interventions of the late twentieth and twenty-first centuries may be seen as a revival, albeit in a less violent form, of yesterday's 'savage wars of peace'. The ultimate goal was similar: fling markets open to the global economy, bring government to the hitherto ungovernable, end tribal conflict and ethnic cleansing, and recruit converts for the West's way of life.

This book is about those earlier clashes of civilizations, wars fought between peoples of radically different mentalities, different levels of political organization and of contrasting technological capabilities. The wars spawned by Western imperialism were more than mere clashes of arms. They were also clashes of culture expressed in the violence of the military idiom. Each Portuguese caravel which, in the fifteenth century, deserted familiar waters to navigate the coasts

Departure of caravels from Lisbon for Brazil, Africa and the East Indies in 1562. The lateen-rigged caravel could sail closer to the wind than any other type of European vessel. It was small enough to sail up river estuaries, yet sturdy enough to withstand Atlantic storms.

of Africa and the seas beyond, was a missile fired in this conflict, a declaration of hostilities in a confrontation the objectives of which were both political and economic. Henry the Navigator's search for Christians and spices kindled a competition between Europeans and indigenous peoples as each attempted to respond to the challenges of new foes and conditions. This competition, and the procession of conflicts it produced, was part of a protracted interaction between the West and the wider world of which the wars of Empire compose a mere chapter. And although it is a chapter the narrative of which appears to be one of irresistible European ascendancy, that ascendancy was hardly an automatic process. 'Victory' was purchased at a cost of significant hardship and occasional failure. And some of those failures were quite spectacular.

From its earliest period, imperial warfare was considered a hazardous and difficult enterprise. Although in the Americas Europeans advanced inland almost from the beginning, their conquest was facilitated as much (if not more) by an advance guard of disease as by military superiority *per se*. And even then, Amerindian hostility meant that frontier posts like Montreal maintained a precarious existence. In the East and in Africa, Europeans remained seabound, clutching a tenuous lifeline to the homeland, content to export spices, gold and slaves from coastal 'factories'.

Three things caused this to change over the course of the eighteenth and nineteenth centuries: political instability in Africa and Asia, European rivalries played out in the wider world, and officers and officials driven by patriotism and personal ambition, eager to claim vast stretches of territory for the fatherland. All of these factors were interrelated. Imperialism was, among other things, the creation of a global economy. The demand for certain commodities – slaves, spices, gold, and eventually sugar, tobacco, coffee, palm oil, furs and opium – touched off economic revolutions in the hinterlands of vast and hitherto self-contained continents. Economic changes soon became political ones as local rulers struggled to control commodities which could be bartered to Europeans. Quite naturally, European nations locked together on a crowded and factious continent, searching for advantage over their neighbours, however marginal, came to view the wealth of the imperial world as a force multiplier, like alliances or technology. Gold from the New World permitted Philip II to raise vast fleets and armies to control an empire which stretched from Antwerp to Lima. Spain's empire did not long remain uncontested, as upstart nations struggled to carve out a market niche, to sever and eventually dominate the sea lanes which were used to flood Europe with the plunder of the Inca, Aztec and Mayan empires and the 'groceries' of the East and the Caribbean. Dynastic rivalries became national ones, and national competition soon personalized into vendettas of honour, ambition and greed among vain and proud men. Imperial expansion, and the wars it spawned, was a cultural clash, certainly. But it was also an enterprise of supremely personal dimensions, a magnification, frequently a mutilation, of the human spirit. Personal ambition – self-confident, gnawing, desperate – became not merely a factor in imperial expansion, but in many cases it was imperialism's primary engine.

Imperial expansion began in part as a series of trade wars. But the term, then as now, is both contentious and misleading. It is contentious because classic liberal theory argues that the words 'trade' and 'war' are incompatible, that trade flourishes in conditions of peace. But that is too simple a view. Many of the early imperialists were merchant adventurers, fighters willing to trade, and traders willing to fight to gain access to markets. All wanted precious metals or spices. The problem was that imperial authorities, operating on theories of mercantilism and narrow, legalistic definitions of empire, tended to view anyone who attempted to breach the restricted bounds of trade regulations as pirates. Therefore, in the colonial context, trade and warfare went hand in hand from the beginning. The process of differentiating a warship from a merchantman was a slow one. Most ships and their crews were expected to be able both to charge a gun and to know the price that silk or tobacco would fetch in London or

Amsterdam. But this changed over time, which is why the term 'trade war' is also misleading. Although trade and economic advantage were to be had abroad, imperialism was not primarily about trade. The merchant adventurer gradually became the naval captain and colonial soldier – Drake and Hawkins transmogrified into Clive, Dupleix, Wellesley (later Duke of Wellington) and Kitchener – and the army of John Company (the East India Company) evolved into a force raised by the government and supported by tax revenue, not company profits.

But merchant or soldier, the problem for all men on the outer edge of the imperial advance was the same: their enemies were many, while their own numbers were inconsequential. As a result, imperial soldiers faced operational challenges of the sort which had confronted Cortés from the moment he fired his boats at Veracruz – how was a relative handful of Europeans with limited technological means to traverse an inaccessible country, to conquer a numerically superior enemy, and pacify a new empire? While these challenges remained difficult, over time European soldiers mastered them to the point that imperial conquest came to be regarded as little more than a technical problem to be solved. For instance, to the end of his career, Wellington, who had directed what was regarded as Europe's toughest fighting in Spain between 1808 and 1813, who had held Europe's fate in his hands in the cauldron of Waterloo, maintained that Assaye, his 1803 victory over Marathan forces, was 'the bloodiest for the numbers that I ever saw', and the best thing that he ever did in the way of fighting. By the end of the nineteenth century, however, the British writer, Colonel C. E. Callwell's classic, *Small Wars,* or the less well-known *Observations sur les guerres dans les colonies,* by the French Lieutenant Colonel Alfred Ditte, could adopt a very prescriptive approach to colonial warfare.

Wars of Empire chronicles the period during which Europeans gradually bested their indigenous foes. That said, however, the image of an irresistible combination of European firepower, discipline and logistics concentrated against sometimes fanatical, but hopelessly outclassed, indigenous forces is a deceptive one. It certainly oversimplifies a more complex interaction of cultural confusion, conflicting political goals and shifting military alliances, not to mention the more stable factors of terrain and technology. The adaptive response of Western soldiers to the challenges of imperial warfare was more apparent in some areas than others, and clearly accelerated as the nineteenth century drew to a close.

This volume will seek to accomplish three tasks: first, to examine the problems posed by the conditions of warfare outside Europe on the European military systems, and how European, and eventually American, soldiers adapted to them. From the earliest days of imperial expansion it was clear to most that warfare outside Europe required special skills and qualities, and that the military organizations of European forces had to prove flexible enough to incorporate those changes while maintaining the advantages of systems developed for war between civilized armies.

Second, as war is an interactive process, European adaptation was conditioned in part by the native response to European invasions. Therefore, one must ask why it was that in most cases, indigenous societies failed to organize a successful resistance. The stock explanation is that native resistance was outgunned. Sometimes – usually, even – it certainly was. However, this book will argue that any theory of imperial advance grounded solely in the technological lag of the defeated is inadequate. While native armies were usually at a technological disadvantage against a European invader, a lack of firepower was not their only, or even their major, disadvantage. On occasion, poorly armed indigenous forces defeated technologically superior European troops because they employed terrain, tactics or surprise to their advantage. British armies fell victim to small Franco-Amerindian forces between 1757 and 1763; to American rebels at Saratoga in 1777 and Yorktown in 1781; to Afghans in 1841–2; and to Indian mutineers in 1857. Chelmsford at Isandlwana in 1879, Hicks 'Pasha' on the Nile in 1883, and Black Week in South Africa in 1899 demonstrated the vulnerability of British commanders who were insufficiently cautious. The French were desperately overstretched during the first decade of the Algerian invasion. They suffered defeat at the Macta Marshes in 1835 and were forced into a devastating retreat from the walls of Constantine the following year. General François de Négrier was sent packing by Chinese forces at Lang Son in 1885, while Lieutenant Colonel Eugène Bonnier's small force was wiped out by Tuareg near Timbuktu in January 1894. The Russians suffered humiliating reversals in the Caucasus in the 1840s. General George Custer's demise on the Little Bighorn in 1876 nearly matched in drama if not in scale that of the Italians at Adowa in 1896. Even the lightly armed Herero people could, on occasion, inflict a reversal on heavily armed German columns, as they did on Major Glasenapp in 1904 at Owikokero in South-West Africa. However, while sometimes victorious in a dramatic battle, these societies were seldom able to sustain lengthy wars against a determined European invader. In fact, the confrontation with a European invader caused problems of adaptation with which indigenous societies were unable to cope.

Retreat from Constantine (Algeria), 1836. Technological superiority cannot account for the success of European arms in the pre-industrial age. Until the advent of magazine-fed rifles and ultimately machine guns, European expeditions into the hinterland of Africa, India or China ran a serious risk of being overwhelmed.

Finally, *Wars of Empire* will conclude with brief observations which contrast the success of imperial soldiers before 1914 with the relative success of indigenous insurgencies after 1918. A detailed study of modern insurgencies is beyond the scope of this work, and will be dealt with in a subsequent volume in the series. This volume is an attempt to preface the problem with the observation that, although imperial military success appeared virtually inevitable and unstoppable before the First World War, in fact it was built on a brittle foundation, both militarily and politically. The tenuous success of imperial conquest before 1914 would become apparent as the First World War was being fought, and even more so in its aftermath.

Even as imperialism rolled forward like an unstoppable juggernaut, clever indigenous commanders like Abd el-Kader in Algeria, Shamil in the Caucasus, Samori in West Africa or de Wet in the Transvaal, despite being poorly armed, were able to resist effectively European encroachment for years, even decades, by engaging in guerrilla warfare. The problem, then, was not one of tactics but one of creating the cohesion in the indigenous society to be able to sustain a war of attrition against the invader, to raise the price of conquest beyond that which he was willing to pay. Because support for imperialism had never run deep in European societies, it was not too difficult after 1945 to convince many imperial countries to vacate the premises; that colonial empires, which, it was now revealed, were vast drains on national exchequers, were simply not worth the effort required to maintain them. In many respects, this was the gift of European imperialism to Africa and Asia. Colonial occupation welded diverse peoples together, gave them the cohesion, if only temporarily, to behave like nations, and educated a leadership capable of focusing national expression and creating a strategy for independence. But that was in the future. To be liberated, empires had first to be conquered. How military men adapted to the challenges of imperial warfare in the eighteenth, nineteenth and early twentieth centuries is the story of this book.

CHAPTER ONE.

The Context:
Why Empire?

*Abd el-Kader proved to be France's
greatest adversary in Algeria. He enjoyed
considerable success from 1832 until
Bugeaud's arrival in 1840. Worn down
by Bugeaud's brutal war of attrition,
abandoned by the Sultan of Morocco
after 1844, Abd el-Kader surrendered
to French General Lamoricière on
23 December 1847.*

The Context: Why Empire?

IMPERIALISM HAS LONG proved a subject of significant historical controversy. That the origins of the historical debate have their roots in the very wars engendered by European expansion is hardly surprising when one realizes that from the beginning, expansion met at best indifference, at worst hostility, in the populations of imperial nations. That hostility acquired an economic rationale when J. A. Hobson, a Liberal MP and economist, denounced the Second South African War of 1899–1902 as a scam perpetrated on the British people by a clutch of patriotic parasites led by Cecil Rhodes. The military resources of England had been mobilized for the personal gain of a few capitalists eager to seize the gold and diamonds of

Cecil Rhodes and the board of directors of De Beer's in 1895. Rhodes' prominence in the exploitation of the diamond mines of South Africa and in the origins of the Second South African (Boer) War (1899–1902) led Lenin to conclude that imperial expansion, and the wars this engendered, were the last gasp of a moribund capitalist system.

South Africa. Why? Because, according to Hobson, home markets were saturated, and capitalists required new territories in which to invest excess capital safely and profitably. It fell to Lenin, however, to lift the specific circumstance of the Boer War into the realm of dogma. While Hobson viewed imperialism as an unproductive economic activity for nations, a movement concocted by conspiratorial confederacies of capitalists to divert vast sums into their own pockets, Lenin insisted in 1916 that imperialism was a logical evolution of capitalism, its 'highest stage'. Capitalists, whose Malthusian policies invariably drove their societies toward social and financial catastrophe, sought to delay the inevitable reckoning through conquests of cheap and reliable sources of raw materials, as well as markets for the products of European industries.

'The Diamond Diggings, South Africa'. This 1872 illustration depicts the free-booting atmosphere that reigned in the diamond mines of the Orange Free State. This was replicated in the Transvaal when gold was discovered there. The influx of British immigrants led to tensions with the conservative Boer population that contributed to the outbreak of war in 1899.

IMPERIAL AGE EMPIRES *c.* 1700

*The New World was exhausted, the trade in 'groceries' – spices, sugar, and coffee –
slaves, fish and furs made fortunes for individuals, but seldom for the merchant
companies that organized the trade nor for the governments that chartered them and
defended their interests.*

The economic dynamism of imperialism was far more evident during the early empires. It was a period when slave labour produced 'groceries' and Amerindians collected furs, and was not an era of wage labour upon which industrial capitalism was based. And even these old empires were largely barren of profit for the nations, even for the

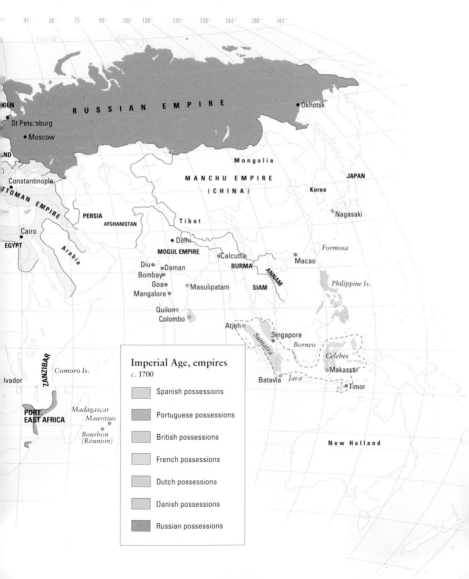

Imperial Age, empires
c. 1700

Spanish possessions

Portuguese possessions

British possessions

French possessions

Dutch possessions

Danish possessions

Russian possessions

merchant companies, which conquered and maintained them. As the British historian of empires, D. K. Fieldhouse, has argued, the mercantilist theory which underpinned the economies of empire was simply old European protectionism extended abroad. Nor, in fact, did mercantilism succeed either as a theory of economic organization or of political control. 'American empires rested on a nice and quite accidental balance between imperial restrictions and the capacity of the colonists to evade them,' he wrote. The result was a financial and administrative burden which allowed Adam Smith to write in 1776 that 'Britain derives nothing but loss from the dominion which she assumes over her colonies'. When Britain attempted to tighten trade restrictions so that she could recoup some of the enormous costs required to administer and defend her North American colonies, she succeeded only in provoking rebellion.

By the nineteenth century, imperialists, at least in Britain, were moving away from mercantilism and toward a system of free trade. The outriders of British expansion to the coasts of China in the mid nineteenth century were businessmen. By demanding open markets free of government regulation or monopolistic restriction, traders like Jardine, Mattheson and Dent helped to transform the emerging imperial consciousness into an ideology that equated free trade with the spread of Western civilization and the rule of law. In this way, imperialism was a revival of the Roman concept of dominion as a moral and military ascendancy over inferior peoples. Merchants were simply to be the initial beneficiaries. But few businessmen saw great profit in the colonies. Capital flowed from Britain and Europe, *not* to the colonies but to North and South America, the white dominions of Australia, Canada and New Zealand, and to develop the gold and diamond mines of the Boer republics. Britain's greatest push to acquire colonies came at the very moment when its economic position had begun to decline. And while some individuals profited from colonial expansion, nations seldom did. In the last years of the nineteenth century the British Empire was a revenue drain. The French paid huge

Hubert Lyautey, an enthusiastic promoter of French imperialism and first Resident General of Morocco in 1912, lamented the fact that the French empire was propped up by government subsidies and military occupation, and remained largely barren of business investment.

subsidies to garrison and develop their unproductive colonies which accounted for less than 10 per cent of French overseas trade by 1900. The future Marshal of France, Hubert Lyautey, lamented in the 1890s that French Indo-China, practically barren of businessmen, was rich in bureaucrats and soldiers. The only German colony which claimed an export worth entering on a balance sheet was Togo, and its palm oil was exploited by British, not German, merchants. The merchant companies which Bismarck hoped in 1884 would manage the German colonies on the model of Britain's East India Company required only one short decade to collapse. By 1914, the German colonial empire cost the German government £50 million in direct subsidies, and probably double that if indirect subsidies and low-interest loans are factored in, against a trade volume of £14 million; it accounted for only 0.5 per cent of Germany's external trade. Indeed, German Social Democrats were fond of pointing out that Germany's trade with Norway was more significant than that with her colonies. While there was a shiver of commercial interest in the British colonies, it weighed lightly in

American naval captain A. T. Mahan's The Influence of Sea Power upon History *(1890) argued that sea control and empire formed the twin pillars of national prosperity. Though Mahan based his argument on the British imperial experience, navalists and imperialists everywhere cited Mahan as a justification for large fleets and imperial expansion.*

Britain's external trade: a mere 1.2 per cent with her tropical colonies at the turn of the century.

Nor does the economic explanation for imperial expansion apply to two other imperial powers: Russia and the United States. The Russian and, until 1898, American empires were continental ones with moving frontiers, and therefore were more obviously military constructions. In each case, settlers and traders had flowed into sparsely populated lands. The state had merely followed. However, by the end of the century, the rationale for each was becoming more obviously economic, similar to arguments made in Britain about the requirement for empire to protect the British worker against foreign competition. In part, the economic arguments began because each country was reacting to events in China. Sergei Witte, finance minister under Tsar Alexander III, sometimes called the 'Cecil Rhodes of Russia', believed at the turn of the century that Manchuria, Korea and Siberia could be squeezed for capital to transform Russia into a first-class industrial power. Likewise, after 1898, American imperialism distinguished itself from the European version, at least in its own mind, because it saw its island colonies as stepping stones to larger markets in China and the Far East, rather than as ends in themselves. That said, the stepping stones did much better out of America, which guaranteed them a secure market for their products, than America did out of her colonies, which were able to absorb only

3.8 per cent of US exports by 1920. Nor did markets in Latin America and China to which the colonies were meant to facilitate access ever prove lucrative. In 1885, for instance, Latin America absorbed only 3.74 per cent of American exports. So, although individual traders, investors and exporters made money in empire, nations never did.

In general, capitalists made indifferent imperialists, and vice versa. The most successful were merchants of death, men who unloaded an estimated 16 million mostly obsolete firearms on Africa in the course of the nineteenth century. Businessmen preferred to deal with established governments, not invest scarce capital in conquest and infrastructure development. Colonies devoured metropolitan subsidies and generated large defence and administrative requirements, against a return of prestige and the distant promise of an economic pay-off.

Imperialism was not the highest stage of capitalism, as Lenin believed, but the highest stage of nationalism. The trouble was that, while imperialists were nationalists, not all nationalists were imperialists. Imperialism's natural constituency was small, confined largely to men of military or journalistic disposition who grasped at empire as an antidote for national decline or as a vision of a new world order. Founded in 1882, the *Kolonialverein* (colonial society) counted 17,000 members by 1889. French colonial groups counted less than half that number, many of whom were schoolboys. Even in Britain, the official mind of imperialism offered a vision by a clutch of leaders who shared similar origins, education and values, rather than an ideology able to unite a mass movement. Imperialists attracted some crossover support on grounds of ideology or group interests: missionaries eager for souls to convert; a handful of businessmen with colonial interests; social Darwinists for whom imperialism offered irrefutable evidence of the survival of the fittest; members of geographical societies who believed exploration a prelude to conquest. A. T. Mahan's *The Influence of Sea Power Upon History*, published in 1890, gave rise to navalism, which on occasion allied with imperialism. Mahan, an American naval captain, equated mastery of the seas with national

The Russo-Japanese War of 1904–5 was the product of the collision of Russian and Japanese imperialism. A fleet-on-fleet engagement in the Tsushima Strait on 27 May 1905 marked the climax of that war and was hailed both as a vindication of Mahan and a preview of the expected naval Armageddon in the North Sea between Germany and Britain.

prosperity, which could be exploited by imperialists who demanded naval bases to protect trade routes and provide coaling stations to give fleets global reach. But as Europe slithered towards war in 1914, navalists focused on fleet-on-fleet engagements, battles of steel-hulled mammoths like that which had helped settle the Russo-Japanese War at Tsushima in 1905, and which they believed would characterize the coming Armageddon in the North Atlantic. Dispatching light cruisers and frigates to occupy islands, or tiny gunboats to navigate malarial rivers to blast half-naked potentates were tasks too modest to extend the attention span of these Dreadnought-besotted patriots beyond the second glass of port.

Benjamin Disraeli, prime minister from 1874 to 1880, purchased a controlling interest in the Suez Canal Company to protect Britain's route to India. He annexed Cyprus, invaded Afghanistan in 1878 and attempted to extend Britain's grip on southern Africa by annexing the Transvaal in 1877, thereby igniting the First South African War.

Because imperialism's support base was limited to pockets of élite opinion, politicians who relied on it for electoral success risked political extinction. No early Victorian prime minister believed that empire was anything other than an accessory to national prosperity and prestige. It is alleged that even Palmerston, a connoisseur of gunboat diplomacy, was unable to locate many of the places where he ordered his navy to intervene on a map. Benjamin Disraeli, prime minister from 1874 to 1880, attempted to elevate empire into a province of the national imagination and, in the process, transform the Tories into the party of empire, forging the link between empire and national greatness in the popular mind. Disraeli's Crystal Palace speech of June 1872 offered the British electorate, swollen in 1867 by the addition of a million working-class voters, a choice between the 'Little England' of the Liberals and an empire of liberty, truth and justice that would make Britain the envy of the world. In 1875 he bought into the Compagnie de Suez to guarantee British control of the Suez Canal, that important link with India and the East, and the following year proclaimed Queen Victoria Empress of India. He travelled personally to Berlin in 1878 to support the Ottoman Empire against Russian encroachment. In the process, he secured Cyprus for Britain as an anchor for Suez and a further stepping stone to the East. However, Disraeli's ministry established the rule that those who live by empire

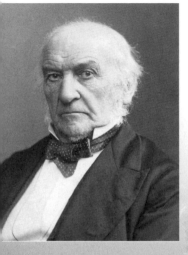

William Gladstone (1809–98), leader of the Liberal Party, demonstrated that imperialism offered a narrow base for electoral success, even in a country like Britain where imperialism was relatively popular. Yet even Gladstone learned that imperial territories, once acquired, were virtually impossible to dispose of.

perish by it. The executioner of Disraeli's imperial strategy was none other than his rival and leader of the Liberal Party, William Gladstone. Gladstone's Midlothian campaign of 1879 offered a denunciation of imperialism as Disraelian theatre, a counterfeit pageant which camouflaged a felonious enterprise. Gladstone denounced the Afghan War of 1878–80 and the Zulu War of 1879–80 as little short of criminal assaults on innocent peoples, helpless against the firepower of Redcoats. 'Remember the rights of the savage!', Gladstone intoned. 'Remember the sanctity of life in the hill villages of Afghanistan, among the winter snows, is as inviolable in the eyes of Almighty God as can be your own!' His invective worked. In 1880, Disraeli crashed in flames and retired.

THE RISKS OF IMPERIALISM

Although Gladstone was the primary beneficiary of Disraeli's fall, he could not escape the burden of imperial unpopularity. He was severely embarrassed by the plight of Charles 'Chinese' Gordon at Khartoum in 1884–5, and suspected that he had been intentionally set up by his colonial proconsul. Moralists lurked, ready to pounce on the inevitable atrocity. Later, the Second South African War nourished a vocal anti-war movement in Britain led by Lloyd George and Emily Hobhouse. And while pro-war nationalists successfully contained them during the war, subsequently governments ran shy of imperial ventures. Liberals cooled on imperialism, while within the emerging Labour Party, imperialism was vilified as a subject of partisan abuse.

If British politicians, secure in the 'splendid isolation' of their island, in possession of the world's greatest navy, found imperialism a hard sell, what could Continental leaders expect but public cynicism.

On New Year's Day 1877 Queen Victoria was proclaimed Empress of India in Delhi in the presence of the Prince of Wales. By associating the royal family more closely with the imperial enterprise, Disraeli hoped to combine the popularity of the monarchy with the pageantry of empire to attract working-class voters to the Tory Party.

The primary concerns of Continental powers were, by definition, European. Imperial conquest was an add-on, a leisure activity to be undertaken only when it did not jeopardize one's fundamental interests at home. Any politician who thought about it for more than

THE BRITISH EMPIRE 1914

It was said that the British Empire had been acquired 'in a fit of absence of mind'. Rather, the process of acquisition in Britain, as for other imperial nations, was a lengthy one driven largely by men on the periphery – explorers, merchants, sailors, soldiers – who gradually claimed, conquered, purchased or suborned pieces of territory which they presented to London as faits accomplis. Once acquired, however, each island and each territory was viewed as a piece of a strategic jigsaw vital for the integrity of the whole.

five minutes should have concluded that he would get little credit when imperial expansion succeeded, and all of the blame when an expedition encountered setbacks. This was true even in France, a country with a long, and at times, glorious colonial history. The launching in 1830 of an expedition to capture Algiers was the Bourbon Restoration's desperate effort to glean popularity from imperial military success. But Algiers' fall failed to postpone that of the Bourbon Restoration, which collapsed in July 1830 in the face of a popular revolution.

The Bourbons were followed by their Orléanist cousins who, after a period of hesitation, adopted a policy of total conquest of Algeria. However, this proved difficult against an enemy who adopted a guerrilla

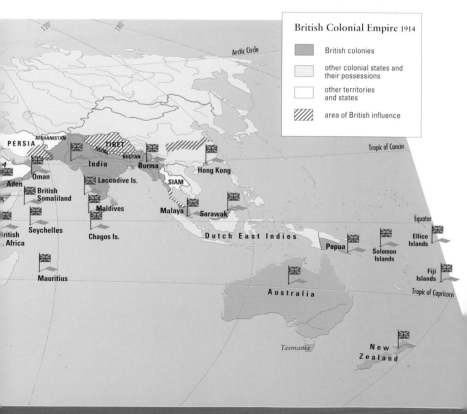

General Thomas-Robert Bugeaud secured an uncertain French mandate over Algeria in the 1840s. While Bugeaud's incorporation of lightly armed troops into mobile flying columns was regarded as tactically innovative, his scorched earth methods employed against Muslims drew criticism in France.

strategy. Therefore, General Thomas Bugeaud, the French commander-in-chief in Algeria from 1841, elevated the *razzia*, or raid, into a strategy of brutal economic warfare against the Muslim population. Soon blackened fields, ravaged fruit orchards and devastated villages marked the passage of French columns. General Castellane, who visited Algeria in this period, defended the *razzia*: 'in Europe, once [you are] master of two or three large cities, the entire country is yours,' he wrote. 'But in Africa, how do you act against a population whose only link with the land is the pegs of their tents? The only way is to take the grain which feeds them, the flocks which clothe them. For this reason, we make war on silos, war on cattle, the *razzia*.'

The growing savagery of the war hit its nadir in June 1845, when Colonel Amable Pélissier trapped a group of Arabs in the caves of Dahra in the coastal mountains north of Cheliff. After desultory negotiations, Pelissier ordered a fire built in the cave mouth. Five hundred Muslim men, women and children were asphyxiated. When Pélissier's report, describing the atrocity in lurid and self-congratulatory prose, was released to the Chamber of Peers, a storm of protest broke out in France. But far from condemning his subordinate, Bugeaud praised Pélissier and even suggested that the action might be repeated. In August of that year, Colonel Saint-Arnaud entombed a large number of Muslims who had sought refuge in a cave: 'There are five hundred brigands down there who will never again butcher Frenchmen,' he trumpeted. Other mass liquidations followed over the next two years. In 1846, Alexis de Tocqueville returned from Algeria horrified by the excesses of the military regime there – he later described the officers of the Algerian army as 'imbecilic'.

The imperial schemes of Napoleon III, which included participating in a joint Anglo-French expedition against China in 1858–60, and a brief flirtation with establishing an Arab empire in the Levant, were stillborn. However, his decision to invade Mexico and use it as a

Louis-Napoleon Bonaparte, the nephew of the great Napoleon, assumed office in 1848 with the idea of extracting France from Algeria. Instead, he became an ardent imperialist, annexing Cochin-China (the southern province of Vietnam), and dispatching troops to Mexico between 1862 and 1867.

springboard to the extension of French influence in Latin America proved to be an unpopular and expensive fiasco which helped to weaken a regime ultimately destroyed by Prussian bayonets. The Third Republic, born in 1870, appeared at first to have learned its lesson about the risks of imperial adventures. It cut colonial expenditure to the bone and concentrated on building up its metropolitan army. However, in 1881, Prime Minister Jules Ferry launched a campaign to seize Tunisia. The political protests that erupted in a country which, Ferry recognized, was disgusted by the imperial adventures of

French Prime Minister Ferry receives the governors of the French colonies. Although one of the Third Republic's most accomplished politicians, he was hounded out of office in 1885 after a minor colonial defeat.

Napoleon III, threw him out of office. His successor, Charles de Freycinet, lost his portfolio when he merely suggested that France might participate with Britain in the suppression of the Egyptian revolt of 1882. Ferry was next hounded from office in 1885 by braying mobs shouting 'Ferry Tonkin!', after French forces suffered a reversal at Lang Son, on the Tonkin-Chinese border. Having repudiated Ferry's policy of expansion in Indo-China, parliament threw out Ferry's successor, Henri Brisson, when he attempted to extend credits to maintain the expeditionary force there.

In many respects, German imperialism was the most eccentric because it was so divorced from Germany's strategic or economic interests. The German empire came about in 1884 as the result of Bismarck's order to his consul in Cape Town to lay claim to South-West Africa and Togo. Later, he recognized the claims made in the name of Germany in East Africa by the German explorer Carl Peters in the mid 1880s. Bismarck's motives continue to baffle historians. He appears to have wanted colonies as diplomatic pawns and to please minority interests. His annexations precipitated the Congo Congress in Berlin of 1884–5, which established the principle of effective occupation as the prerequisite for colonial claims, and in the process touched off the great African land rush which dominated

Carl Peters (1856–1918) pressed inland toward the Great Lakes region to claim what was to become German East Africa, claims later acknowledged by German Chancellor Otto von Bismarck. According to Lord Salisbury, the arrogant attitude of 'cheap and nasty officials' like Peters provoked the 1888 revolt in German East Africa.

Otto von Bismarck's 1884 decision to lay claim to African lands caught his contemporaries by surprise. The subsequent Berlin Congress of 1884–5 established the principle of 'effective occupation' of a territory before it could be claimed, touching off the great imperial land rush that Jules Ferry called 'the steeplechase to the unknown'.

In this 1889 lithograph, the leader of an uprising in East Africa is executed by German marines. The conquest of imperial populations was often a source of dissension both within countries and between them. However, by wrapping themselves in the banner of nationalism, imperialists could surmount the problem of fragile popular support for imperialism.

the last two decades of the century. Whatever his motives for claiming pieces of Africa, the German chancellor rapidly lost interest in imperial expansion, especially when the chartered companies which he believed would administer the colonies either failed to materialize or went bust. The disillusionment with empire was fixed in 1904–6 with the brutal suppression of the Herero and Maji-Maji rebellions in South-West Africa and German East Africa. The Reichstag was dissolved in 1906 after opposition politicians protested against the brutality of these wars by refusing to vote in the budget. In the aftermath of this crisis, Chancellor Bernhard von Bülow created a colonial office and undertook to create a corps of professional administrators to avoid a repetition of such public relations disasters.

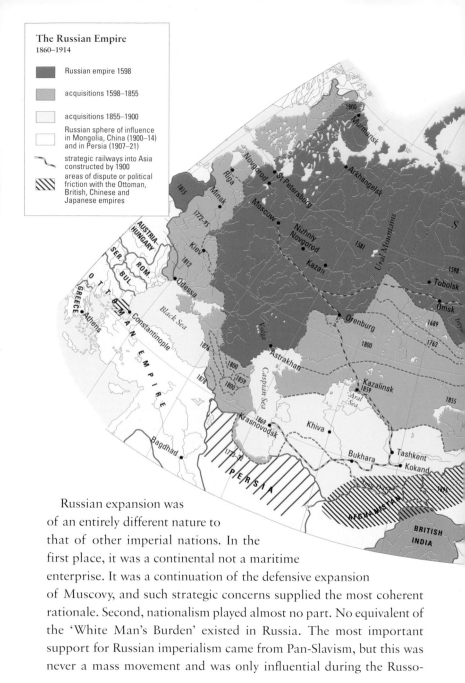

The Russian Empire
1860–1914

Russian empire 1598

acquisitions 1598–1855

acquisitions 1855–1900

Russian sphere of influence
in Mongolia, China (1900–14)
and in Persia (1907–21)

strategic railways into Asia
constructed by 1900

areas of dispute or political
friction with the Ottoman,
British, Chinese and
Japanese empires

Russian expansion was
of an entirely different nature to
that of other imperial nations. In the
first place, it was a continental not a maritime
enterprise. It was a continuation of the defensive expansion
of Muscovy, and such strategic concerns supplied the most coherent
rationale. Second, nationalism played almost no part. No equivalent of
the 'White Man's Burden' existed in Russia. The most important
support for Russian imperialism came from Pan-Slavism, but this was
never a mass movement and was only influential during the Russo-

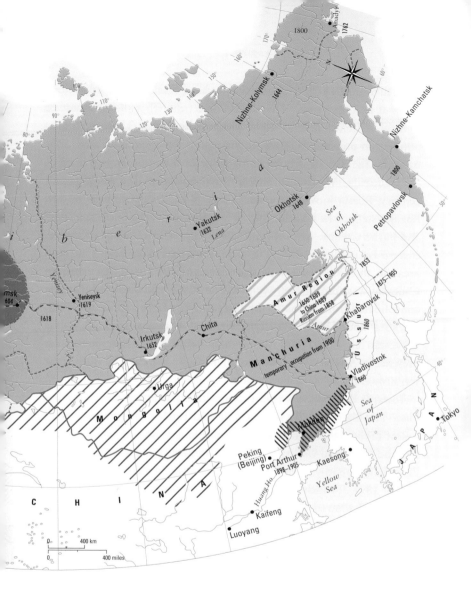

THE RUSSIAN EMPIRE 1860–1914

Russia's was a continental, rather than a seaborne, empire. It expanded largely because, with the exception of the Caucasus, it met minimal resistance. That would change in the early twentieth century as the collapse of China brought Russia into conflict with Japan in Manchuria and Korea.

relations would come to replicate tumultuous European ones. Finally, Mahan and the navalists argued for keeping the islands to serve as coaling stations on the route to the markets of Asia. Intellectually, then, the United States was receptive to empire.

'Colonel' Theodore Roosevelt led a troop of volunteer 'Rough Riders' in Cuba in 1898. As US president from September 1901, Roosevelt assured American control of the Panama Canal, sent troops to the Dominican Republic (1905) and to Cuba (1906), and mediated the end of the Russo-Japanese War in 1905, for which he was awarded the Nobel Peace Prize.

The groundwork for American expansion beyond its shores had also been laid politically. William Henry Seward, the Secretary of State who purchased Alaska in 1867 and annexed Midway Island in the same year as a strategic base for Pacific expansion, is often seen as the founder of American imperialism. Nevertheless, when, in 1892–3, Americans in Hawaii overthrew the monarchy there and demanded annexation, President Grover Cleveland hesitated as annexation went against the wishes of the Hawaiian people. However, the tide began to turn with the election of William McKinley in 1896. But when Washington suddenly found itself in possession of islands as the result of the defeat of Spain in 1898, no one quite knew what to do with them. Cuba was occupied, and later abandoned to a new regime. Few Americans knew where the Philippines were, or even what they were – one senator thought they were canned goods. But the usual reasons were evoked as an excuse to maintain them under American control – if America did not take the Philippines, Germany or Japan would. Like Hawaii, the Philippines offered stepping stones and naval bases to extend US trade and influence to the East. Missionaries, forgetting or ignoring that the Philippines were already Catholic, wanted to secure them for Christianity. The acceptance of a seaborne empire confirmed the views of those who

William Seward's purchase of Alaska and annexation of Midway Island in 1867 as a basis of Pacific expansion made him, in the minds of many, the father of American imperialism.

argued that America must take its place as a world power, an extension of Manifest Destiny beyond the shoreline. American theorists became like men of religion who, having preached the virtues of evangelical poverty, suddenly discover the benefits of ministering to a well-heeled parish. They had to work overtime to harmonize their capitalist, anti-imperialist dogma with preferential tariffs and the moral dilemma of ruling subject peoples.

Once empire was acquired, its retention acquired a strategic rationale. Historians have concluded that an official mind of imperialism formed in Britain, a strategic awareness that vital choke points along the route to India and the Far East must remain under British control. And while Paris was also aware that its interests in Algeria and Indo-China also had strategic requirements, British historian Christopher Andrew has suggested that the imperial mind in France was purely unofficial – reluctant, reactive, and a hostage to Gallic xenophobia. And because the chancelleries of Europe were peopled on the whole by reluctant imperialists, imperialists *malgré eux*, for the most part, they reacted to initiatives undertaken by men on the periphery which they appeared practically powerless to control. Men, mainly soldiers, expanded the bounds of empire without orders, and often against orders. This was a phenomenon as old as imperialism itself. It was difficult, if not impossible, to control the expansion of empire. In London, Paris, St Petersburg, or Berlin, many ministers knew little of the places conquered and cared less. Empires were often appallingly administered, allowing those with energy and initiative a freedom limited only by the ability of indigenous peoples to resist their encroachment.

Much of British expansion in India occurred during the French Revolutionary and Napoleonic wars when the British government was otherwise preoccupied. Although the Industrial Revolution gradually closed the communications gap, European capitals were still weeks, if not months, distant. When, in 1843, General Sir Charles Napier executed, by his own admission, 'a very advantageous, useful, humane piece of rascality' to capture Sind in the climactic battle of Hyderabad, *Punch* magazine suggested that the only battle report which could convey a proper sense of remorse would be the Latin *Peccavi* or 'I have sinned'. Of course, Napier was no more remorseful than was his French contemporary Bugeaud, who informed his government in 1847 that he intended to advance the frontiers of French control in Algeria into the Kabylia despite orders to the contrary. 'It is obvious that I must take the full responsibility,' he wrote, 'I accept it without hesitation.'

By the late nineteenth century, French soldiers had become masters of deception, failing to inform Paris of their advances, even altering maps and place names to camouflage their conquests from prying politicians. When, for instance, in 1903, French General Hubert Lyautey moved from Algeria to occupy the Moroccan city of Bechar, he promptly renamed it Colomb 'to spare diplomatic susceptibilities'. Indeed, government orders to inhibit military action could actually precipitate it; in 1912, when a wire arrived from Paris forbidding Lyautey from seizing Marrakesh, the French commander folded it, slipped it into his back pocket, sat down and ordered General Charles Mangin to seize Marrakesh. He 'received' the wire only after Mangin entered the city. Although the German case is somewhat different, in that Bismarck ordered German representatives to lay claims to South-West Africa, Togo and the Cameroon, he did choose to acknowledge the treaties signed in the name of the German Empire by the explorer Carl Peters in East Africa in the 1880s. Russian expansion in Central Asia was a series of military *faits accomplis* – 'General Chernyaev has taken Tashkent,' Interior Minister Valuev noted in July 1865, 'and nobody knows why.'

In short, beneath the sermons of missionaries, the schemes of traders, and the pride of nationalists in the vastness and virility of empire, imperialism boiled down to a military phenomenon encouraged by a vocal but numerically insignificant minority. To understand the dynamic of imperial expansion, one must examine its primary component – imperial warfare.

CHAPTER TWO

Colonial Warfare in the Pre-Industrial Age

Circassians repel Russians near Achatl in 1841. Mountain warfare limited the advantages of technology, and required tactical skills that the Russians were slow to master in the Caucasus.

Colonial Warfare
in the Pre-Industrial Age

IN 1896, C. E. Callwell published *Small Wars*, a book which offered an almost encyclopedic survey of wars that pitted European armies against weak, irregular opponents, beginning with Hoche's suppression of the Vendée revolt during the French Revolution. Callwell was well placed to comment on the development of imperial warfare. Of Anglo-Irish extraction, schooled at Haileybury (which specialized in educating the sons of colonial soldiers and civil servants) and the Royal Military College, he was commissioned into the Royal Artillery in 1878. He fought in the Afghan War of 1880, and the First South African War in the following year. After passing through the Staff College in 1886, he served five years in the intelligence branch of the War Office. It may have been in these years that Callwell began collecting his notes for *Small Wars*.

Small Wars was destined to become a minor classic of military literature. It reflects the era in which Callwell wrote, the 'high renaissance' of imperialism. By the end of the nineteenth century, the advantage in small wars had swung definitively in the invader's favour. Yet it had not always been so. Until the mid nineteenth century, imperial soldiers were seldom more advantaged in technology than Cortés, with his tiny arsenal of firearms, three centuries earlier. Indeed, in the East especially, European invaders were at best only equal to their opponents, and sometimes even inferior in firepower against an indigenous enemy able to produce his own muskets and artillery.

In colonial North America, the British had few if any qualitative technological advantages over their Amerindian, French or American opponents. Indeed, early on, the adaptive response of Amerindians to technological change outstripped that of the European arrivals. The transition from the bow and arrow to flintlock was a natural one for Amerindian men adept at hunting game, shooting at individual targets,

Amerindians examine weapons in a Hudson's Bay Company trading post in 1845. Indigenous peoples seldom had a problem acquiring modern weapons in the pre-industrial age, so long as they had trading goods of value to exchange.

and raised in a warfare culture that placed principal value on stealth and surprise. Amerindian life was a permanent mobilization, a perpetual *lévée en masse*. Young men were eager to join proven war leaders for ambushes and raids whose ostensible purposes were to dominate weaker neighbours, extort tribute, extend hunting or fishing rights, control trade or avenge an insult. But the real goal was prestige, and this flowed to those who closed with the enemy, often with club or axe: 'all that are slain are commonly slain with great valour and courage,' wrote the New England pioneer Roger Williams, 'for the conqueror ventures into the thickest, and brings away the head of his enemy.'

Against the warfare culture of Amerindians, technology gave the colonists only marginal advantage. The folklore of the deadeyed marksmanship of intrepid North American frontiersman is mainly just that – a myth. In Europe, weapons were a quasi-monopoly of the landed classes and poachers, so that few colonists were expert in their use upon arrival. In some marginal agricultural areas like New France, some colonists chose the unencumbered life of the *courreurs de bois* or 'mountain men', followed the fur trade and lived as did the Amerindians. In New England, however, agricultural and artisan pursuits allowed scarce time to acquire hunting and marksmanship skills equivalent to those of the Amerindians. Nor was there any need to learn, as Amerindians proved more than willing to earn extra cash by selling venison and turkey to settlers, or by shooting wolves who preyed on livestock. Archaeological excavations suggest that hunting game other than birds was infrequent, at least in the New England colonies.

So while Amerindians were quick to adopt the flintlock musket, the persistence among Europeans in North America of the matchlock, inferior to the bow and arrow for hunting but adequate for the volley-firing drills of village militias, disadvantaged the new arrivals well into the seventeenth century. The longevity of the matchlock was also encouraged in some measure by the sentiment that taking aim at individuals was neither chivalrous nor Christian. Efforts by the colonists to staunch the technological transfer of muskets and later rifles to the indigenous population inevitably collapsed because the English, French and Spanish, thin on the ground, were forced to arm Amerindian allies. Also, traders were eager to swap weapons for furs in the north, and deerskins, Apalachee horses and Amerindian slaves in the south. Amerindians also learned to repair weapons and manufacture shot, after edicts placed that market off-limits to colonial craftsmen. Their biggest lacuna, however, was powder, which was not manufactured in North America but had to be imported. In this respect, the end of the French and Indian War in 1763 severely curtailed Amerindian resistance, for it dried up their alternative sources of powder. Even in the Second Seminole War which began in 1835, American soldiers complained that their smooth-bore muskets were of little use against Seminoles armed with rifles. The downside of improved technology for Amerindians was an escalation in lethality. The acquisition of weapons to protect against rival tribes made fights to control the fur trade or to protect the village from merciless settler encroachment literally struggles for survival. Amerindian combat increased in desperation as both muskets and friction with colonists transformed indigenous warfare from a largely ritualistic demonstration in personal courage into something close to total war.

Seminoles ambush supply wagons escorted by US Marines at 12-Mile Swamp near St Augustine, Florida in 1812. The thick, jungle-like foliage of central Florida made the enemy difficult to locate and rendered artillery virtually useless.

Before the introduction of the breech-loading rifle in the 1860s, matching Europeans in firepower posed little problem in the Far East. The states of India could manufacture their own muskets, powder and bullets, and even artillery at a pinch. Indian sepoys who turned their weapons against their employers in 1857 did not fail for lack of arms – on the contrary, the British were positively shot to pieces at places like Cawnpore and Lucknow. The Mutiny failed for lack of good leadership, nor was there an ideology powerful enough to unite India's many ethnic and religious groups into a unified movement.

The French in Algeria discovered, in the 1830s, that their short-range muskets offered only a marginal defence against long-barrelled and longer-range Arab *jezails*. The mountaineers' mastery of tactics, rather than small-arm superiority, made the invasion of the Caucasus a

Calvary for the Russians. In 1854, Turks and English shipped late-model rifles to Shamil in the hope that he would draw off Russian forces from the Crimea. But by then, Shamil's rebellion had begun to show serious signs of disintegration. The Brown Bess and the 1777 model Spanish musket were favourites in the South American war for independence. But humidity and lack of powder and flints compounded the usual inefficiency of these weapons, to the point that executing prisoners by firing squad was regarded as a profligate expenditure of precious munitions. Among South American Indians fighting for both sides, clubs and even poisoned arrows remained the weapons of choice. Skirmishes in the Andes were often won by the side which could gain the high ground and roll boulders down on the opposition. Not a shot was fired in anger during the penultimate battle of the war, fought at Junin in August 1824, which was exclusively an affair of the *armes blanches* (swords). The Tokolor empire of al-Hajj Umar, which by the 1860s stretched from Senegal to Timbuktu, used the gold of West Africa to purchase arms in Sierra Leone, and recruited Africans from European colonies to serve as soldiers and gunsmiths.

Artillery might give the invaders an advantage, but not invariably so. Two brass field cannon hoisted up the cliffs on to the Plains of Abraham helped Wolfe to gain victory over Montcalm, who attacked before his artillery – indeed, before the bulk of his force – was in place. Wellesley discovered that 6-pounders, which he distributed two per battalion, were particularly effective in India because the enemy tended to swarm in dense, target-worthy packs which dissolved in bloody panic after a few discharges of grapeshot. He also found artillery useful in attacking Indian fortifications like Tipu's capital at Seringapatam, which were low-walled and poorly designed, as were those of Central Asia besieged by Russians in the mid nineteenth century. Artillery allowed the French to seize Constantine in 1837, although the defenders inexplicably mined their own curtain wall, thus allowing the French to storm through the breach. But battles were seldom decided on the basis of superior firepower – Marathan and Sikh forces were well supplied with artillery, for example, although heterogeneous and eccentrically organized, and employed European instructors to train their gunners in the latest European techniques. English volunteers organized artillery regiments in Venezuela after 1817. Artillery gave Bolívar an important edge against royalist troops at Pichincha in May 1822. Russian deserters, many probably Polish or Georgian, manned Shamil's artillery in the Caucasus. In 1857, Indian mutineers unsportingly kept the artillery for themselves, so that subsequently the British admitted only white soldiers into that arm. In 1858, artillery prevented al-Hajj Umar's 20,000 *sofas* (warriors) with their siege ladders from approaching the walls of the French fortress at Medine on the Senegal river, a bloody failure which initiated the decline of the Tokolor empire.

However, the remoteness of imperial battlefields invariably made artillery something of a liability, especially the heavier variety employed

The retreat from Constantine, 1836. The square, a standard tactical formation in European warfare in the early nineteenth century, survived in colonial warfare into the twentieth century. However, indigenous fighters usually required only one defeat before they understood the futility of attacking squares, and reverted to guerrilla tactics.

in the eighteenth and early nineteenth centuries. If the weight of gun carriages were reduced for mobility, only a few rounds could be fired before the wood began to split. If the carriages were solidly designed, mobility became a problem – forty bullocks and a female elephant were required to haul one of Wellesley's 18-pounders in India. Getting a siege train to Constantine in 1836, and again the following year, required considerable logistical effort, which is one reason why Bugeaud limited the artillery in his flying columns to two guns when he became commander-in-chief in Algeria in 1840. But more important, Bugeaud discovered that the offensive spirit of his troops diminished in direct proportion to the defensive firepower of their artillery. 'You drag thousands of wagons and heavy artillery with you which slows your movements', Bugeaud told the officers under his command. This was going to change: to begin with, 'no more heavy artillery, no more of these heavy wagons, no more of these enormous forage trains. The convoys will be on mule back and the only cannons permitted will be light ones'. So disturbed were Bugeaud's officers by a new order of battle, which looked to them more like a recipe for collective suicide, that they delegated the senior colonel to talk their new commander out of this folly. Bugeaud sent him packing. Americans in the Seminole Wars found artillery effective as a means of softening up Amerindian villages as a prelude to a bayonet attack – if they could find the villages! In open warfare, the thick, jungle-like foliage of central Florida simply absorbed the shot of light mountain guns. The difficulties of manhandling artillery through remote Caucasus passes was such that, in 1845, General Vorontsov was forced to destroy his guns when most of his artillery horses had died. The only guns he kept were light field and mountain guns, developed especially for use in the Caucasus and introduced in 1842.

The real technological edge enjoyed by the West in this period was naval. There was no real equivalent in the non-Western world to Europe's naval superiority, which bestowed at least three advantages on the invaders. The first was power projection. If Europe discovered the world from the fifteenth century, and not vice versa, it was because the capability in the form of well-built ships had married the motivation to sail forth and conquer. Navies gave the West strategic reach, a means of passage to the most distant corners of the earth opposed only by the caprice of nature and the ships of rival European navies. As A.T. Mahan noted in *The Influence of Sea Power Upon History*, 'if Britain could be declared the winner in the imperial race, the credit, or blame, resided with the superiority of the Royal Navy'. A second benefit of naval superiority for imperialists was security. In the early days when Europeans were on the defensive on land, especially in Africa and the East, they seized coastal enclaves, often islands like Goa, St Louis de Senegal, Hong Kong or Singapore, which they could defend and supply by sea. Precarious frontier posts like Montreal might have succumbed to Amerindian constriction had their communications depended exclusively on overland routes.

Finally, sea power meant operational and even tactical mobility, which could translate into strategic advantage. Sea power was the force multiplier for the British. The British ability to shift their troops up and down the coast in India was an important element in their victory over the French there. In 1762, British maritime expeditions sent to punish Spain for her alliance with France in the Seven Years War seized both Manila and Havana. In North America, the Royal Navy gave Britain the decisive edge over France, a country with three times the population and ten times the army. Maritime expeditions swept up French settlements around the Bay of Fundy in 1710, captured Louisbourg in 1745 (and again in 1758), and imposed a blockade which, by stemming the supply of gunpowder, munitions and muskets, began the unravelling of France's Amerindian alliances as far inland as the Great Lakes, the Ohio Valley and Louisiana. A seaborne strike in 1759, behind a screen of men-of-war blockading French ports, allowed Britain to pierce the heart of New France at Quebec, rescuing what, until then, had been a fumbling campaign of attrition against the southern glacis of French Canada. And although the French Navy –

British General Wolfe's troops scaled the cliffs from the St Lawrence river to the Plains of Abraham in 1759 to attack Quebec from the land side. Two brass cannon helped to deliver victory against a French garrison that rushed from the walls to give battle before it was fully mustered.

to Sainte Foy

Plains of Abraham

French Army

British Army

3

to Sillery

1

to Anse au Foulon

The Battle of Quebec

The Royal Navy extended the reach of British imperial power and gave London a decisive edge in eighteenth-century Franco-British imperial wars. France's relative maritime inferiority invariably challenged Paris's ability simultaneously to protect its far-flung empire in India, the Caribbean and North America during the Seven Years War. Both Louisbourg on Cape Breton Island and Quebec fell to British seaborne expeditions. La Royale returned the compliment at Yorktown in 1781.

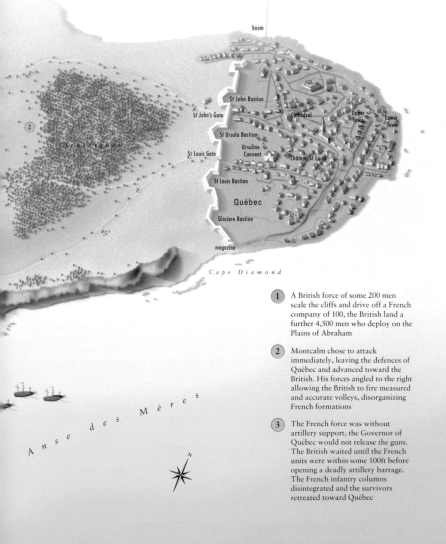

boom

St John Bastion

St John's Gate

Cathedral

Upper Town

Lower Town

St Ursula Bastion

St Louis Gate

Ursuline Convent

Château St Louis

St Louis Bastion

Québec

Glaciere Bastion

magazine

Cape Diamond

S t   F o y   R o a d

2

Anse des Méres

N

1 A British force of some 200 men scale the cliffs and drive off a French company of 100, the British land a further 4,500 men who deploy on the Plains of Abraham

2 Montcalm chose to attack immediately, leaving the defences of Québec and advanced toward the British. His forces angled to the right allowing the British to fire measured and accurate volleys, disorganizing French formations

3 The French force was without artillery support, the Governor of Québec would not release the guns. The British waited until the French units were within some 100ft before opening a deadly artillery barrage. The French infantry columns disintegrated and the survivors retreated toward Québec

La Royale – returned the favour twenty-two years later at Yorktown, sea power had made land operations against New France a leisurely march to a foregone conclusion. British maritime expeditions had harvested so many islands of the French Antilles by 1762 that British diplomats attempting to negotiate a peace were embarrassed by their nation's military success. British sea power forced Napoleon to abandon the reconquest of Saint Domingue (Haiti) in 1803.

Dominance of the Pacific was essential for the victory of the rebellious South American colonies, who promoted Lord Cochrane, a disgraced Scottish aristocrat, to the rank of admiral, and launched a successful amphibious assault on Lima, an oasis in the desert, from

Valparaiso in Chile in 1820. Foreign corsairs organized a small fleet to assault Spanish ships in the Caribbean.

Brown-water operations were also a feature of imperial warfare. Lake Champlain and the Richelieu river provided a classic invasion route into and out of New France. During the Second Seminole War, the United States Navy operated steamboats on the larger rivers while oared, flat-bottomed Mackinaw boats, capable of carrying twenty, moved men along the tributaries. This permitted American

Seminole chief Osceola led a tenacious insurgency in central Florida in the 1830s. However, United States troops and volunteers regained operational mobility through the use of flat-bottomed Mackinaw boats on the numerous rivers and tributaries of the region, and by luring away former Black slaves fighting with Osceola with promises of freedom.

British frigates approach Canton on the Pearl river during the Opium War of 1839–42. Chinese junks were unable to prevent British vessels from attacking coastal fortifications, or from cutting the vital Grand Canal that carried much of China's north–south trade. British smugglers quashed Chinese efforts to keep opium out of the country.

troops and volunteers to re-establish their presence in central Florida, abandoned to the Seminole chief Osceola in 1835. Without the support of the Russian navy, the string of posts along the Black Sea created to sever supplies from Turkey to Shamil would undoubtedly have fallen to Murid attacks. Following the Crimean War, these maritime outposts served as bases of operations against the Cherkess population of the western Caucasus. British victory in the Opium War with China (1839–42) demonstrated how relatively small naval forces could impose their will even on a vast continental empire. Sea power allowed the British to transform what the imperial court in Beijing viewed as a distant dispute in Canton into a struggle which directly threatened the economic health and political stability of the empire itself. Junks and poorly defended Chinese coastal fortifications offered scant defence against twenty-five Royal Navy ships of the line, fourteen steamers, and nine support vessels carrying 10,000 troops. With this relatively small force, the British seized four important coastal trading centres, sailed up the Yangtze river to block the Grand Canal which carried much of the

Celestial Empire's north–south commercial traffic, and threatened Nanking. This was enough to bring the Chinese to the peace table. However, in 1884–5 the French were far less successful in employing their navy to wring concessions from the Chinese when they attacked Formosa which, clearly, Beijing did not believe vital to its interests. The creation of a gunboat force was critical in allowing the Celestial Empire to defeat the Taiping and Nien rebellions, sparked by European encroachment, in the 1860s. Naval artillery made the walled cities held by the Taipings along the Yangtze untenable. Gun sampans and eventually gunboats on the Yellow river and Grand Canal escorted grain convoys, and linked a defensive chain of fortifications created to keep Nien forces from breaking out across the Yellow river, much as the British in the Boer War of 1899–1902 used railways to link barriers of blockhouses built to contain Boer commandos. The French pioneered river flotillas to advance up the Senegal river toward the Niger from the 1850s.

By the end of the nineteenth century, Callwell could write that while climate and terrain ceded strategic advantage to the enemy, tactical advantage invariably fell to the invaders. In the pre-industrial period, however, the invaders might not even possess a tactical advantage, especially if the indigenous enemy declined to fight in a manner that favoured the close-order drill of Western armies of the period. Ambush was the tactic of choice of Amerindians, who noted that English colonists moving through the forest 'always kept in a heap together, so it was as easy to hit them as to hit a house'. Lacking European notions of chivalry, they regarded a white chief, distinguished by his clothing and his horse, the prime target. The colonists, with their leaders down and a substantial number of their comrades killed or wounded by Amerindians concealed in the bush, were often too disorganized to recover from the initial surprise. For General Edward Braddock, this came as the ultimate lesson in July 1755 on the Monongahela, when his East Anglian and American troops were swarmed upon, decimated and their remnants put to flight by a small expedition of French frontiersmen and their Amerindian allies untutored in, and unintimidated by, the

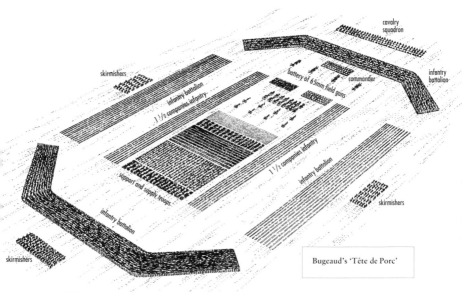

The following labels appear on the diagram:

cavalry squadron

skirmishers

battery of 65mm field guns

commander

infantry battalion

infantry battalion

1½ companies infantry

1½ companies infantry

infantry battalion

support and supply troops

skirmishers

infantry battalion

skirmishers

Bugeaud's 'Tête de Porc'

THE 'TÊTE DE PORC'

Bugeaud's 'pig's head' formation delivered a victory when Abd el-Kader impetuously attacked it on the Sikkak river in 1836. Most imperial armies adopted a variant of this formation, which offered an all-round defence and shielded the vital convoy in hostile territory. In practice, however, such tight formations were difficult to maintain in broken or wooded terrain (see page 119).

shoulder-to-shoulder volley-firing tactics of the Anglo-Saxons. The power of these volleys might be diminished also because soldiers tended to skimp on powder to lessen the force of the musket's recoil.

Bugeaud, who first went to Algeria in 1836, criticized the French for forming massive squares of up to 3,000 men, several lines deep. Arabs seldom attempted to overwhelm squares, and the men in the interior ranks were wasted because they were unable to fire. Instead, he advocated small squares with overlapping fields of fire to give mutual support. Volleys, he believed, should be regular, and firing withheld for as long as possible to allow the enemy to get close enough to do him real damage. In 1836, Bugeaud achieved a major victory when he formed his troops into a 'pig's head', and marched them on to a plateau above the Sikkak river. Bugeaud's formation confused the Arabs, because it offered no vulnerable front or rear guard to attack. When they threw themselves at the French, they were repulsed by massed musket fire, made more deadly by a technique perfected by harassed French troops in Spain. A musket ball was cut into four parts and rammed down the barrel on top of the already introduced ball to create a sort of small-arms grapeshot – very useful against an enemy that liked to work in close, at knife-point. Bugeaud then ordered his men to drop packs and attack, driving a large number of Arabs over a bluff to their deaths in the Sikkak river below. Another 500, cornered at the foot of a rock outcropping, surrendered, the first time the French had bagged so many POWs in Algeria.

When Europeans had triumphed in these set-piece battles, as at Assaye in 1803, at the Sikkak river in 1836 or at Isly in 1844, it was superior discipline and tactics rather than firepower that assured their victory. Indeed, in India Wellesley's favorite tactic was to loose a single volley followed by a charge. The trouble with European tactics, especially successful applications of them, was that the enemy quickly learned not to fight Europeans on their own terms. Bugeaud's success

on the Sikkak was not repeated because his opponent, Abd el-Kader, now knew better than to rush massed French troops. By refusing battle, drawing an invading force deep into the country where it became overextended and vulnerable, an intelligent enemy might negate European tactical superiority. A reversal, even a withdrawal after a successful operation, could be costly. 'If you were forced to retreat through these people, you could be certain of having them constantly around you,' the Hessian Johann Ewald remembered of the American Revolution, a memory no doubt shared by Burgoyne and Cornwallis. The French discovered as much in Algeria at the Macta Marshes in 1835 and the following year at Constantine, as did the British in Afghanistan in 1842. In the Caucasus, Shamil became expert at

Last stand of the 44th at Gandamak. The disastrous British retreat from Kabul in 1842 was fairly illustrative of what might happen to imperial forces retreating through hostile territory, increasingly slowed by casualties and fatigue, vulnerable to well-crafted ambushes. This was a fate shared on occasion by British forces in North America, the French in Algeria and the Russians in the Caucasus.

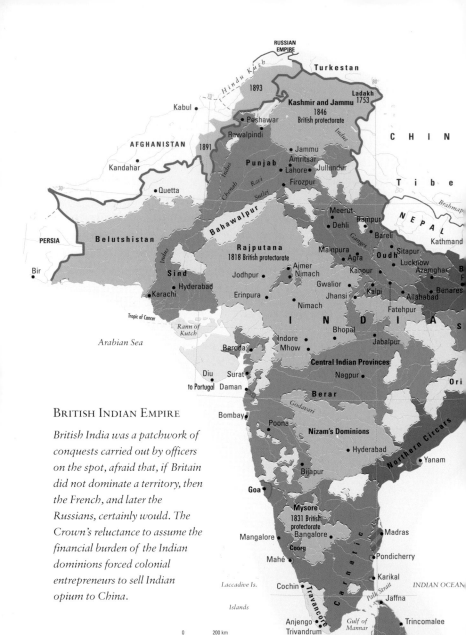

RUSSIAN
EMPIRE

Turkestan

Hindu Kush

1893

Ladakh
1753

Kabul

Kashmir and Jammu
1846
British protectorate

Peshawar

Rawalpindi

Indus

C H I N

AFGHANISTAN

1891

Jammu

Kandahar

Amritsar

Punjab

Jullundur

Lahore

Firozpur

T i b e

Quetta

Chenab

Ravi

Sutlej

Indus

Brahmap

Meerut

Dehli

Rampur

N E P A L

PERSIA

Belutshistan

Ganges

Bareli

Kathmand

Rajputana
1818 British protectorate

Mainpura

Oudh

Sitapur

Bir

Ajmer

Nimach

Agra

Lucknow

Kanpur

Azamghar

B

Sind

Jodhpur

Gwalior

Kalpi

Benares

Karachi

Hyderabad

Erinpura

Jhansi

Allahabad

Nimach

Fatehpur

Indus

Tropic of Cancer

*Rann of
Kutch*

I N D I A

S

Bhopal

Jabalpur

Arabian Sea

Baroda

Indore

Mhow

Central Indian Provinces

Nagpur

Ori

Diu

to Portugal

Surat

Daman

B e r a r

Godavari

BRITISH INDIAN EMPIRE

*British India was a patchwork of
conquests carried out by officers
on the spot, afraid that, if Britain
did not dominate a territory, then
the French, and later the
Russians, certainly would. The
Crown's reluctance to assume the
financial burden of the Indian
dominions forced colonial
entrepreneurs to sell Indian
opium to China.*

Bombay

Poona

Nizam's Dominions

Hyderabad

Yanam

Northern Circars

Bijapur

Goa

Mysore
1831 British
protectorate

Bangalore

Madras

Mangalore

Coorg

Pondicherry

Mahé

Karikal

Carnatic

Laccadive Is.

Cochin

Travancore

Palk Strait

INDIAN OCEAN

Islands

Jaffna

Anjengo

Trivandrum

*Gulf of
Mannar*

Trincomalee

Kandy

Colombo

Ceylon
1798 to Britain

0   200 km

0   200 miles

allowing the Russians to meander through valleys, sacking town after deserted town, and then cutting them to ribbons when they attempted to return to base, as was done following the Russian victory at Akhulgo in the eastern Caucasus in 1839. Shamil's great triumph, however, came in 1845 as Prince Vorontsov's flying column withdrew through the Chechnian forests toward his base. The Russians were able to cover only 30 miles in one week, in the process abandoning baggage and wounded and losing 3,321 men, 186 officers, and three generals to Shamil's attacks. Similarly, Osceola kept American forces off-balance with well-crafted ambushes during the Second Seminole War.

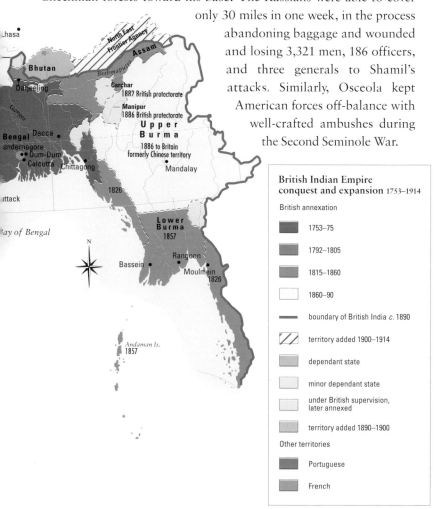

**British Indian Empire
conquest and expansion** 1753–1914

British annexation

- 1753–75
- 1792–1805
- 1815–1860
- 1860–90
- boundary of British India *c.* 1890
- territory added 1900–1914
- dependant state
- minor dependant state
- under British supervision, later annexed
- territory added 1890–1900

Other territories

- Portuguese
- French

Without obvious technological or tactical advantage, the best commanders sought to give themselves what in twentieth-century terms would be called an 'operational edge'. The foundation of Wellesley's success in India was organizational. Earlier commanders in India like Clive had fought close to base because they lacked the logistical capacity to strike deep into the enemy heartland. In India, as elsewhere in colonial warfare, it was an axiom that a large force starved while a small one risked defeat. On his arrival in India, Wellesley discovered that British expeditions resembled migrating people rather than an army. As many as 20,000 troops organized in a single force lumbered over the countryside, averaging 10 miles on a good day, but requiring one day's rest in three, and forced to meander to find food and fodder. Wellesley recognized that strategic success could result only after his army was reorganized along

lines that would allow greater mobility. In his campaign against Dhoondiah in Mysore, Wellesley divided his forces into four armies, which kept his opponent guessing and allowed the British to march up to 26 miles a day to achieve surprise.

Wellesley's experience was repeated elsewhere as French, British, American, even Russian and Chinese commanders moved to light or flying columns – Hoche used them in the Vendée and Bugeaud in Algeria. Indeed, when he returned to Algeria as Governor General in 1840, Bugeaud was nearly overwhelmed by a sense of

India proved a valuable training ground for Sir Arthur Wellesley, the future Duke of Wellington. Wellesley's success, like that of Bugeaud in Algeria, relied principally on his organization and tactical methods, rather than on technological superiority. He maximized the use of strategic surprise by increasing the mobility and striking power of his forces.

déjà vu – the French army was repeating the mistakes which this Napoleonic veteran had seen it make in Spain during the Peninsular War. Most of the soldiers were tied down to fixed positions and tormented by the Arabs who raided their supply wagons and destroyed crops and supplies behind the lines. Attempts to launch reprisal raids faltered in the absence of any clear objectives. Columns of thousands of men, weighed down by artillery and supply wagons, toiled over a stark and blistered countryside in search of their foe. The enemy retreated before them, refusing battle but slashing at flanks, supply convoys, and stragglers. After a few weeks of campaigning in this manner, French expeditions, like Russian ones in the Caucasus in the same period, would return to base exhausted, with very little to show for their efforts.

Bugeaud set out to remodel his listless and demoralized command: 'we must forget those orchestrated and dramatic battles that civilized peoples fight against one another', he proclaimed to his troops, 'and realize that unconventional tactics are the soul of this war'. Bugeaud based his reforms on four principles: mobility, morale, leadership and firepower. In place of fortifications, which had been the principal French method of controlling the countryside, he emphasized the value of scouting parties and intelligence reports in locating enemy forces against which troops could be rapidly deployed. Mobile columns numbering from a few hundred to a few thousand men, shorn of artillery and heavy wagons, could fan out over the countryside to converge from different directions on a previously selected objective. In this way, Bugeaud was able to penetrate areas that before had been immune to attack, carry the fight to the enemy and give them no rest. But Bugeaud's mobility, like that instilled by Wellesley in India, depended on sound operational innovations. The medical services were reformed to improve the health of his troops. Equipment was redesigned, and the load of the foot soldier considerably lightened; supplies were carried by mules instead of men or wagons. His light columns were expected to survive by plundering the grain silos or raiding the flocks of the Arabs.

Abd el-Kader's smala, *or extended entourage, was surprised by French troops commanded by the Duc d'Aumale in May 1843. This was an outcome of Bugeaud's 'search and destroy' tactics carried out by mobile 'flying columns' shorn of artillery and other impedimenta, with supplies carried by mules rather than by men or on wagons.*

Light columns were not invariably a formula for success. Without good intelligence, columns might wander the countryside, striking into thin air. They also defied military wisdom by dividing one's forces in the face of the enemy. The division of forces was a less risky option in the imperial context, however, as the enemy seldom had the capacity to overwhelm well-armed troops. However, this was not invariably so. A mobile enemy might easily concentrate against the weakest column, as the Americans discovered in the Seminole Wars, the French in Algeria, and the Russians in the Caucasus.

Of course, in war tactics and operations are for naught if the strategy is flawed. British General Sir Garnet Wolseley encouraged colonial commanders to seize what the enemy prized most. Callwell counselled offensive action and dramatic battles because he believed it the best way to demonstrate the 'moral superiority' of the European. This worked best against a foe with a fairly cohesive system – a capital, a king, a standing army, a religious bond – some symbol of authority or legitimacy which, once overthrown, discouraged further resistance. But that was easier said than done. Indigenous societies might be too primitive to have a centralized political or military system, or to assign value to the seizure of a city like Algiers or Kabul. Insurrections against both English and Spanish rule in the New World began in the cities. However, the ability to control major cities did not win the war for either power, and in fact weakened them by forcing them to scatter their forces. Shamil would pull his population deep into the mountains and force the Russians to attack fortified villages organized in depth, while he simultaneously slashed at their greatly extended supply lines, a tactic which Mao successfully replicated against Chiang's 'encirclement' campaigns of the early 1930s. And while the Russians might eventually take these villages after desperate fighting, their casualties were such that victory was gutted of strategic significance and they were inevitably forced to retreat through hostile country. The French quickly seized most of the towns in Mexico soon after their invasion in 1862. But that merely caused them to spread their forces in penny packets and gave the Mexican resistance virtually a free hand to roam the countryside, concentrating and striking at will against isolated French garrisons. So, the towns might become prisons for invading armies rather than bases for offensive operations. Yet, urban centres often had to be defended because the fall to the rebels of a town like Philadelphia or Lima would invariably be hailed by the insurgents as a measure of progress toward victory.

A charismatic leader might be important to the success of the resistance, but his capture or death would seldom by itself collapse opposition. One can speculate about the destinies of the revolutions in North and South America had Washington or Bolívar been neutralized, thus eliminating a symbol, a strategist, and a set of political skills required to keep insurrection alive. Certainly, Toussaint L'Ouverture's treacherous capture in 1803 while he was dining with French General Charles Leclerc, failed to extinguish the island rebellion. On the other hand, although the 1857 Mutiny is regarded by Indian nationalists as an expression of popular resistance to British rule, it failed largely because it lacked a leadership and a nationalist ideology capable of uniting diverse social and religious groups. Many, if not most, Indians preferred British government to domination by indigenous rivals. French pressure, which forced Abd el-Kader to seek refuge in Morocco from 1843, did not put an end to Algerian resistance. In Abd el-Kader, French officers created a symbol of a unified conspiracy against imperial advance. In doing so, they credited the Arab leader with an authority over his own people that he probably did not possess. Shamil's leadership dramatically increased the effectiveness of resistance in the Caucasus between 1840 and 1845. But, with or without Shamil, the Caucasus offered the Russians nothing but the prospect of desperately hard campaigning. Over time, Shamil's presence actually began to benefit the invaders as it fragmented his following of independent mountaineers, especially the less fanatical Cherkes in the western Caucasus, who chafed under his draconian discipline and Murid beliefs, and who opposed Shamil's attempts to establish a family dynasty by having his son recognized as imam. Decapitating the leadership might even prove counterproductive, because it shattered the opposition into a host of petty chieftains who had to be dealt with piecemeal, as Wellesley discovered in India after the death of Tipu.

Most resistance movements in the pre-nationalist period were no more

Abd el-Kader proved a formidable opponent for the French from 1832 to his capture in 1847. In the long run, however, his Algerian insurgency, like most resistance movements, proved to be a fragile coalition of tribes and sub-chiefs which a clever European commander might split with a combination of force and incentives.

than fragile coalitions. The wise commander, like Wellesley, realized that the most effective method of conquest was political, that the resistance must be offered a reward for submission beyond that of the sheer terror of the alternative. Wellesley was fairly lenient with Hindu *polygars* who ruled from hill forts, allowing them local autonomy so long as they accepted British policy and did not deal with the French. Outside areas of substantial colonial settlement, like Mediterranean Algeria, the French favoured a policy of indirect rule, appointing *caids* or chiefs willing to do their bidding, although as the century progressed they tightened their administrative grip on their colonial dominions. This was a policy forced on the invaders by necessity, as they seldom had the capacity to occupy and police the entire country. Even the Russians, in the wake of Vorontsov's disastrous 1845 campaign, realized that they would not win the Caucasus by force of arms alone. They began to restore the powers of tribal leaders jealous of the authority lost to Shamil, curtail the introduction of Russian law, customs and immigrants, allow native courts to adjudicate tribal disputes, and cultivate economic relationships. Although these policies were applied inconsistently and little influenced the heartland of resistance, they fragmented Shamil's coalition on the margins and pacified base areas so that the Russians could free up more troops for offensive operations.

Because the Americas were, from the beginning, colonies of settlement, alliances between the indigenous population and the invaders could be no more than temporary ones. American mythology holds that the early colonists survived because they adopted Amerindian agricultural techniques. They did more than that – they also adopted and adapted native war tactics. In seventeenth-century New England, colonists discovered military disaster was best avoided by employing Amerindians to act as scouts, allies in combat, and instructors in tactics. The Connecticut Council advised the Bay Colony 'to grant [the Amerindian allies] all plunder, and give them victuals, with ammunition, and a soldier's pay during the time they are out'. But suspicion of the loyalties of indigenous peoples accused of selling their

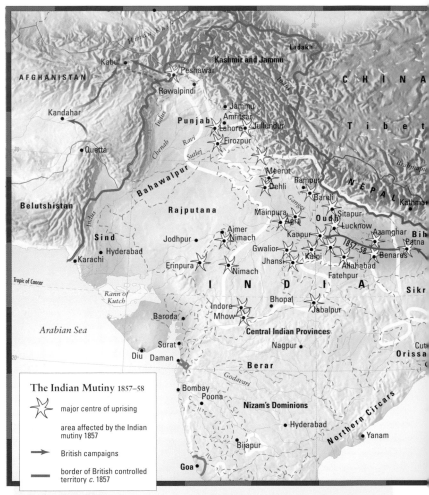

The Indian Mutiny 1857–58

✳ major centre of uprising

area affected by the Indian mutiny 1857

➡ British campaigns

━ border of British controlled territory c. 1857

The Indian Mutiny

Although the Mutiny is seen by Indian nationalists as the expression of an emerging national conscience, in fact its failure demonstrated the absence of a spirit of national resistance to British encroachment. A spontaneous, leaderless uprising, it failed for lack of support among a heterogeneous people, many of whom preferred British rule to that of Hindus or other indigenous groups.

powder, warning their fellow Amerindians of an approaching column, and of desultory fighting, and a persistent belief that skulking modes of warfare were dishonourable, died hard in New England. Unlike their Yankee counterparts, however, English colonists in the south showed few qualms about organizing war parties numbering in the hundreds for war against the Spanish and French along the Gulf Coast, or against troublesome tribes, the pay-off for assistance being the swarms of captives which their Amerindian allies could ransom or sell as slaves.

Amerindians did have their limitations as soldiers and allies. Colonial wars of conquest were decided by sieges, set-piece battles and sea power, not by the guerrilla tactics of ambush and raid. The 1,200 Amerindians serving with the French at Quebec in 1759 saved neither the town nor the empire for France. Many colonial commanders concluded that Amerindian allies were more trouble than they were worth, and encouraged the development of ranger units of white frontiersmen. Expeditionary forces in the French and Indian wars, the North American offspring of the Seven Years War, were volatile mixes of regular European, colonial volunteer and Amerindian forces who shared neither political goals, tactical methods, nor common notions of discipline. Amerindians might be useful on the margins of a campaign in the same way that partisans supported main force action in European war: for example, had he bothered to recruit them, Amerindian scouts might have diverted Braddock from decimation at the hands of a Franco-Amerindian force half his size on the path to Fort Duquesne (Pittsburg) in July 1755. It was the French, however, outnumbered in the North American theatre, who had greater need of Amerindians than did their British opponents. This created a dependence which could be as fatal as having no Amerindian auxiliaries at all. Braddock's disaster was in part offset by the failure of the French counter-offensive against Fort Edward in September 1755. The French commander, Baron Dieskau, found his Amerindian allies reluctant to invade English territory, and positively mutinous when he ordered them to assault fortified English positions. Amerindians viewed the European preference for sieges as wasteful and having little to do with the real goals of war, which were to enhance personal honour and wealth by taking scalps and seizing captives. Formalized conventions of European warfare were so incomprehensible to them as to border on the grotesque. When, for instance, the Marquis de Montcalm accorded the garrison at Fort William Henry the honours of war in 1757, the 2,000 or so Amerindians, who had been mere spectators to the siege, pounced on the English prisoners, killing and scalping over 200 men.

No fools, the Amerindians also realized that contact with Europeans brought fevers and death. Amerindians stayed away in droves from French expeditions during the smallpox years of 1756 and 1758, a factor which helped to keep the French on the strategic defensive. One result of the Anglo-French wars was to lessen the combativeness of the tribes. Evidence suggests that, after 1755, Amerindian allies of both French and British had come to a tacit agreement not to fight each other, precisely the same charge levelled against them by

ANGLO-FRENCH STRUGGLE FOR NORTH AMERICA

Franco-British conflict was a permanent feature of warfare in eighteenth-century North America to the fall of Quebec in 1759. Both sides enlisted Amerindians to dominate the fur trade and as allies in war. In the end, sea power and the larger population tilted the advantage to the British.

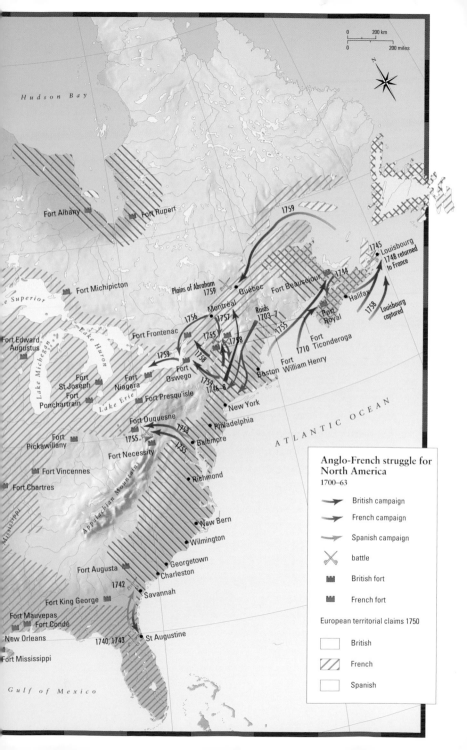

Hudson Bay

Fort Albany
Fort Rupert

1759

1745 Louisbourg
1748 returned
to France

Fort Michipicton

Plains of Abraham
1759

Québec
Fort Beauséjour
1744

Lake Superior

Montréal
1756
1757
Raids
1703-7

Halifax
1758
Louisbourg
captured

Fort Edward
Augustus

Fort Frontenac
1755
1758
1755
Fort
Royal
1710

Fort
Ticonderoga

Lake Huron

1759
1758

Lake Michigan

Fort
St Joseph
Fort
Pontchartrain

Fort
Niagara
Fort
Oswego

1759
1746-8

Fort
William Henry

Boston

Lake Erie
Fort Presqu'isle

New York

Fort Duquesne
1758
Philadelphia

ATLANTIC OCEAN

Fort
Pickawillany
1755
Baltimore

Fort Necessity
1755

Fort Vincennes

Richmond

Fort Chartres

New Bern

Appalachian Mountains

Wilmington

Fort Augusta
Georgetown
Charleston

1742

Fort King George
Savannah

Fort Mauvepas
Fort Condé

New Orleans
1740, 1743
St Augustine

Fort Mississippi

Gulf of Mexico

0   200 km
0   200 miles

N

Anglo-French struggle for North America
1700–63

→ British campaign

→ French campaign

→ Spanish campaign

⚔ battle

🏰 British fort

🏰 French fort

European territorial claims 1750

☐ British

▨ French

☐ Spanish

New England colonists a century earlier. In the short term, the combination of disease and an agreement to pull their punches hurt the French more than the British, for New France was more dependent on Amerindian support than were the English colonies.

The real value of recruiting Amerindians was political and psychological, not tactical. Amerindian resistance to European encroachment was in reality a series of temporary and fragile coalitions of groups who shared scant notion that survival lay in co-operation. Recruiting some of their number fragmented their response and helped to demoralize diehard resisters. In the 1830s, the Seminoles were brought to heel in part by recruiting friendly Seminoles and Creeks, and by enticing Black slaves who had joined the rebellious Amerindians into the service of the US army against the promise of freedom. Not only did this deprive Osceola of much of his military capability, as Blacks were among his best military leaders, but acting as scouts from 1836, ex-slaves also led General Thomas Sidney Jesup to the Seminole villages whose destruction, together with the treacherous capture of Osceola and other Seminole chiefs under a flag of truce, helped to cripple the resistance.

Examples of successful indigenous resistance were few, even in the pre-industrial era. The victory of the American revolutionaries, while impressive, was facilitated by powerful French and Spanish intervention, which, for the British, reduced North America to a secondary front in an Atlantic war. Whether or not the American revolutionaries could have won without French intervention is an open question. But French support in the form of cash, an expeditionary force, and naval assistance gave heart to the insurgents and speeded the conclusion of the hostilities by co-ordinating Cornwallis's defeat at Yorktown in 1781. Yorktown may be termed a decisive victory, even though the war limped on for another two years, for it convinced the British to cut their losses on an indecisive North America front, and to salvage their Caribbean and Mediterranean assets.

In some respects, Toussaint L'Ouverture's rebellion against the French in Saint Domingue can be seen as the most spectacular and successful of

Toussaint L'Ouverture was a remarkable politician and general. Nevertheless, Toussaint's victories depended on the contingent circumstances of French disarray caused by the Revolution, yellow fever which decimated the French army, and British sea power which forced the French to lift their siege of the island in 1803.

slave rebellions which became a permanent feature of the Caribbean once Africans were imported to replace Arawaks in the sixteenth century. Runaway slaves, called Maroons, were able to defend remote and inaccessible islands or portions of islands and of the South American mainland against white attempts to reclaim them. These rebellions were led by African warriors captured in battle and sold by African potentates into the backbreaking work of the canefields. As forests disappeared under the relentless progress of sugarcane cultivation after 1700, Maroon bands survived only on the larger islands like Cuba, Puerto Rico and Jamaica. So fierce was Maroon resistance on Jamaica that in 1738 Governor Edward Trelawney was forced to recognize two Maroon homelands on the island. A similar situation prevailed on Saint Domingue where the French governor signed a treaty with a Maroon named Le Manuel, whom he could not defeat, who had occupied the forested highlands between Saint Domingue and Spanish Santo Domingo. But in general, slave rebellions, even spectacular ones like that which controlled the Danish islands of Saint John for six months in 1733 and the 1760 revolt in Jamaica which required a year and a half to quell, while violent, were short lived.

Toussaint L'Ouverture's success resided in a number of contingent factors quite apart from his talent as a general. First, French legislation and practice had, since the beginning in the 1730s, increasingly alienated the élite of mixed-race Creoles – of which Toussaint was a member – from the island's White establishment, thus splitting a White–Coloured alliance that was critical in keeping slaves in check on other islands. Second, the French Revolution of 1789 provoked a civil war among Whites on the islands. As government authority collapsed, a slave rebellion broke out near Cap Français on August 1791 and quickly spread. Third, a French governor, Léger Sonthonax, arrived in September 1792 who, firm in the Jacobin conviction that the White planters were royalist reactionaries, allied with the Coloured militias against the Whites. As civil war raged on the island, in June 1793, Sonthonax, desperate for support, declared the abolition of slavery, a local initiative confirmed by the National Convention in Paris on 4 February 1794. Blacks rallied to Sonthonax. Offered a choice between death or exile, most of Saint Domingue's 30,000 Whites fled.

In London, a group of Saint Domingue planters persuaded Prime Minister William Pitt to dispatch a British army of 20,000 soldiers to Saint Domingue. This initiated an inconclusive five-year intervention in which a rump of French troops, Spanish soldiers from Santo Domingo and the British battled for control of the French portion of the island through the haze of a malaria-ridden campaign. Toussaint, a Creole slave from the North Province, manoeuvred adroitly among the warring factions, first having allied himself with the Spanish who helped him recruit a force of 4,000 Blacks, and then casting his lot with the French in 1794. By the following year the Spanish had retired to their half of the island. In 1798, British General Thomas Maitland tired of Toussaint's guerilla tactics and sailed away with the feverish remnants of his force. Toussaint then turned his army, which numbered around 55,000 Blacks, against the Coloured militias in the south.

A French force of 20,000 Swiss and Polish conscripts returned to re-establish French rule in February 1802. Toussaint was captured and perished miserably in a French dungeon in April 1803. Saint Domingue's brief flirtation with independence might have ended there had it not been for the combination of French political blunders and British sea power. The re-imposition of slavery by the French sparked a vicious rebellion among a population otherwise exhausted by war and alienated by Toussaint's heavy-handed and authoritarian government. As in North America, a combination of fierce local resistance led by Toussaint's lieutenants, which the French Army, decimated by yellow

The French freed the slaves on Saint Domingue in 1793, and then made the mistake of reversing course under the influence of Josephine, Bonaparte's wife and a native of Martinique. Former slaves on Saint Domingue offered no quarter to French-led troops sent to reimpose servitude on them in 1802.

South American Revolutions
c. 1820

Spanish territory *c.* 1800

Portuguese territory *c.* 1800

1810   date of independence

1817   date of separate statehood

Spanish territory after 1830

●   Spanish base up to 1826

British territory

British claimed

French territory

Dutch territory

independent American state

→   Simon Bolivar's campaign of 1822–4

→   San Martin's campaign of 1817–22

British North America

jointly occupied by US and Britain

disputed with Britain

UNITED STATES OF AMERICA

0   600 km

0   600 miles

N

M E X I C O

1821

Tropic of Cancer

Mexico City   ● Veracruz

Cuba

Belize

UNITED PROVINCES OF CENTRAL AMERICA
1839 dissolved
1823

Jamaica

HAITI

Puerto Rico

Guadeloupe
Dominica
Martinique

● Caracas

Trinidad

REPUBLIC OF NEW GRANADA 1831

VENEZUELA
1811 1820

Surinam

Guiana

PACIFIC OCEAN

Bogotá ●
1811 1830

REPUBLIC OF GREATER COLOMBIA

claimed by France

ECUADOR
1822 1830
● Quito

● Manaus

● Belém

EMPIRE OF BRAZIL

1822
Independent from Portugal

Salvad

P E R U

● Lima   1821

BOLIVIA

● La Paz   1825

Rio de Janeiro

PARAGUAY
1811

Tropic of Capricorn

Antofagasta

São Paulo

Asunción

to Chile

UNITED PROVINCES OF LA PLATA
1816

URUGUAY
1828

Santiago

Mendoza

ARGENTINE CONFEDERATION
from 1825–53

Montevideo

to Chile   1818 CHILE

Concepción

Ancud ●

P a t a g o n i a

1820 occupied by Brazil
1825–8 disputed between Bra
and Argentina
1825 declared its independen
1852 recognized

SOUTH ATLANTIC OCEAN

Islas Malvinas
1770–1820 Spanish
1820–33 Argentine
1833– British

fever, was unable to master, and the appearance of a British fleet in the summer of 1803 precipitated a French withdrawal. Jean-Jacques Dessalines, one of Toussaint's generals, proclaimed Saint Domingue independent under the name of Haiti, an aboriginal word meaning 'the land of the mountains', and promptly assumed the title of emperor.

Latin American rebels successfully threw off the yoke of Spain, aided in part by over 5,000 English soldiers of fortune who imported many skills into Bolívar's army and navy. But the retention of her South American colonies was simply beyond the power of a country devastated by the Napoleonic invasion of 1808 and by the civil war which followed. When insurrection erupted in 1817, only 10,000 Spanish troops garrisoned the widely dispersed South American ports. Madrid was able to spare only 27,000 reinforcements by 1821, and as many as two-thirds of these quickly succumbed to tropical diseases. Insurrection in Spain, touched off by soldiers at Cadiz in 1823 who refused to embark for the colonies, meant that the defence of Spanish interests was shouldered principally by South American royalists. And while some of these men proved able commanders, their focus was local and their troops tended to desert if they were marched beyond their recruitment area. While Bolívar was able to devise a strategic vision for the independence movement, which covered all of South America, Madrid's strategy could only be reactive, defensive and unco-ordinated.

Other imperial resistance movements, with the possible exception of Afghanistan, were less successful in persuading the invaders that the

SOUTH AMERICAN REVOLUTIONS c. 1820
Several factors contributed to the success of the South American independence movement. Among them were a Spanish mother country debilitated by war and occupation during the Napoleonic Wars and hence unable to apply sufficient repressive force; Bolívar and San Martín, two charismatic leaders able to supply a strategic vision to the rebellion; and last, sea power contributed principally by British sailors demobilized after the Napoleonic Wars, which supplied strategic mobility and logistical support to the rebellion.

game was not worth the candle. Abd el-Kader gave the French a good innings, as did Shamil the Russians. But both were ultimately ground down and defeated. In Mexico, the Juaristas ultimately succeeded in expelling the French in 1867. But French intervention of 1862 must be viewed in the context of a long-running civil war between conservatives and reformers in Mexico. Napoleon III's intervention had been possible in the first place only because the United States, engulfed in a civil war of its own, was unable to prevent it. The forces of intervention, which included French, Austrian and even Egyptian troops, never numbered more than 37,000, too few to occupy such a vast country. Napoleon III counted on local support, or indifference, and initially received enough of both. Indeed, there had been no popular uprising when the United States invaded Mexico in 1848. The Mexican population was generally content to allow the Mexican–American War to remain a clash of regular forces and did little to harass the lengthy supply columns of the invading American armies. However, the French succeeded in provoking a national insurrection where the United States had failed. By creating a throne for the Austrian, Maximilian, Louis-Napoleon demonstrated that his goals for Mexico extended far beyond those of the United States, which had laid claim only to the sparsely populated north and whose forces withdrew immediately after the cessation of hostilities. Nor could Mexico nurture hope of outside support for continued resistance against the United States. Hardly had the ashes of the Confederacy gone cold in 1865, however, than Napoleon III came to realize that he was desperately overextended. Washington began actively to stimulate the insurgency with an infusion of surplus weapons and immigrants, many of whom were demobilized soldiers, freed Black slaves, or simply bandits eager to profit from the growing chaos south of the border. The French army was largely light infantry, organized to fight in Algeria where horses were expensive and relatively rare. As a result, the French were unable to cope with the gangs of mounted guerrillas who, taking advantage of their strategic mobility, dismantled France's control over the Mexican countryside and locked them into scattered towns. French attempts to take to horseback, and recruit mounted units of Amerindians with cadres drawn from the Foreign Legion, were too little too late. Still, one may argue that the decisive battle for Mexico was won by the Prussian Army at Königgrätz in 1866, for it served notice that France needed to repatriate its army to prepare for a showdown with Prussia.

Even in the pre-industrial era when they had a better chance to match, even best, the invaders technologically and numerically, few societies were able to do so. One adaptive response, given the obvious superiority of European discipline and methods of warfare, was to modernize local forces to match European standards of skill and professionalism. In India, the process of creating armies on a Europeanized model began in imitation of the Sepoy units created by Clive and Dupleix during the Seven Years War. Many of these units, under the command

of European or half-caste soldiers of fortune, achieved respectable levels of proficiency in the Indian context. But against a European opponent, even one relying to a large degree on its own locally recruited units, they appear to have been at a disadvantage because the Indian potentates proved reluctant to alter their semi-feudal social structure to accommodate a modern army. So Indian armies,

Sepoy was a corruption of Sip-ah, Persian for army. British, French and Portuguese in India recruited native soldiers who were gradually organized into formal regiments. Without indigenous troops, the imperial powers would have been unable to conquer and maintain their vast empires.

though superficially modernized, lacked a coherent officer corps and administrative structure to support them. Worse, in the case of the Sikhs, for example, the new army became such an intrusive political force that some Sikh *sidars* or lords actively conspired to have it defeated by the British.

Chinese efforts to modernize to meet the Western challenge in the first six decades of the nineteenth century were also stillborn. Modernization was bound to be an uphill task in an empire imbued with an unshakeable faith in its own superiority over the barbarian, a profound ignorance of foreign realities, and a belief that defeat was the consequence of moral decline, not material weakness. The emperor was a father figure, the 'Son of Heaven', whose task was to issue moral pronouncements to his people. Civil servants were scholar officials, who grew long fingernails and spent their days writing poetry and mastering calligraphy. Their reports to the emperor were in the form of memorials, which the emperor perused for errors in calligraphy and composition. Confucianism, which emphasized a harmonious social order of hierarchy and status, was the ideology of empire. Any attempt to introduce efficiency into this traditional system, to convince the emperor to drop his pretensions, initiate normal diplomatic relations, and promote men able to administer and lead modern armies inevitably rocked it to its very foundations, for it challenged the moral basis of the regime.

Chinese forces at the outset of the Opium War of 1839–42 consisted of twenty-four *Banners* stationed at strategic points throughout the country. These were understrength

CHINA, DRUG WARS AND REBELLION 1840–1873

Western encroachment into China from the early nineteenth century, especially the sale of opium by force, exposed the Ch'ing dynasty's weakness. Western governments humiliated the throne in its people's eyes, then propped it up against the inevitable internal rebellions this provoked.

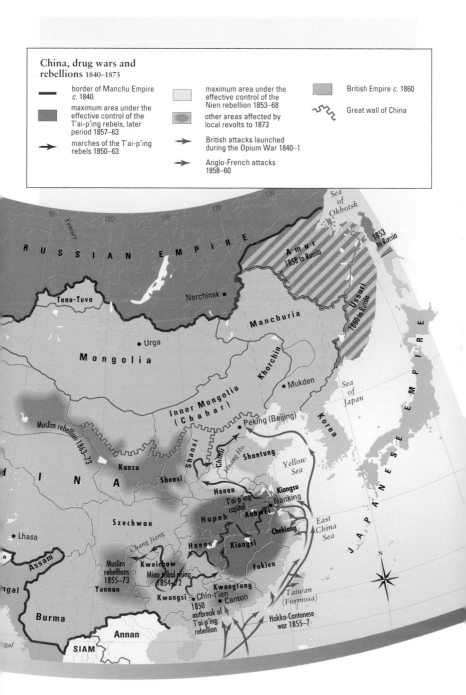

China, drug wars and rebellions 1840–1873

— border of Manchu Empire *c.* 1840

■ maximum area under the effective control of the T'ai-p'ing rebels, later period 1857–63

→ marches of the T'ai-p'ing rebels 1850–63

□ maximum area under the effective control of the Nien rebellion 1853–68

● other areas affected by local revolts to 1873

→ British attacks launched during the Opium War 1840–1

→ Anglo-French attacks 1858–60

■ British Empire *c.* 1860

⌇ Great wall of China

RUSSIAN EMPIRE

Yenisey

Tanu-Tuva

Nerchinsk •

Sea of Okhotsk

1853 to Russia

Amur 1858 to Russia

Ussuri 1860 to Russia

Manchuria

Khorchin

• Mukden

Sea of Japan

• Urga

Mongolia

Inner Mongolia (Chahar)

Peking (Beijing) •

Shansi

Chihli

Huang Ho

Shantung

Korea

Muslim rebellion 1863–73

Kansu

Shensi

Honan

T'ai-p'ing capital

Nanking •

Kiangsu

Yellow Sea

Szechwan

Chang Jiang

Hupeh

Anhwei

Hunan

Kiangsi

Chekiang

• Lhasa

Muslim rebellions 1855–73

Kweichow

Miao tribal rising 1854–72

Fukien

East China Sea

Assam

Yunnan

Kwangsi

Kwangtung

• Chin-tien

Canton

Taiwan (Formosa)

Bengal

Burma

1850 outbreak of T'ai-p'ing rebellion

Hakka-Cantonese war 1855–7

JAPANESE EMPIRE

Annan

SIAM

CHINA

and largely independent companies of poorly disciplined peasants, whose training consisted of formalized sword drill, and who posed more of a threat to the peasantry than to the enemy. They were useful for internal control, but incapable of forming an expeditionary force to deal with the British threat. No surprise, then, when in 1840, the governor of Canton, Lin Tse-hsu, was confronted by a British invasion, he evinced little faith in the regular army. Instead, he recruited local militias, imported Western arms, and even a modern ship, after British frigates blew seventy-four Chinese junks out of the water in the Pearl river. He translated foreign newspapers to assess foreign reaction to the British encroachment. Imperial officials were horrified. The traditional Chinese response in the face of a barbarian who possessed clear military superiority was to appease: manipulate him with a combination of trade and gifts, demonstrate the superiority of Chinese culture, and convince him to perform the *kowtow*, thus acknowledging the imperial view of the universe. The militia threatened their ability to do this, and were largely regarded as 20,000 troublemakers. In their view, the demands of the militia recruits to fight the British would escalate the conflict and result in a disastrous defeat. Chinese commanders attributed British military success not to their own incompetence or weaknesses, but to the presence of large numbers of traitors in their own population. Lin was dismissed, the militias disbanded, the British were paid an indemnity and given an extended lease on Hong Kong Island as a secure base for the opium trade. Other Western countries demanded, and received, equal treatment, which included the admittance of missionaries, and treaty ports, to include Canton and Shanghai, from which they could trade free from the reach of Chinese law. The British and French intervened for a second time in 1858–60 to force the Chinese government to live up to their trade agreements.

The Opium War was followed in China by the Taiping rebellion (1851–64) and the Nien War (1851–68). While these were not, strictly speaking, imperial conflicts in the sense that Western forces did not directly confront Chinese ones, the wars were a direct consequence of the destabilization of China sparked by the Opium War and the imposition of the unequal treaty system on the Ch'ing dynasty. They also offer a test case for the failure of modernization in China, as Western powers followed an ambiguous and contradictory policy there. On the one hand, they periodically intervened in China to force the government to accept extraterritoriality and other unfavourable treaty conditions. Then, having done their best to undermine the credibility of the Ch'ing dynasty in the eyes of the Chinese population, they hastened to bolster its military strength through technological upgrades, advisers and occasional naval intervention so that it could master the subsequent popular uprisings provoked by Western encroachment. The Taipings were pseudo-Christians who swept up landless peasants, Triads (a secret society ostensibly dedicated to a Ming restoration, but which degenerated into gangsterism), and members of militias disbanded in the wake of the Opium War. Some 120,000 strong by 1852, they seized Nanking as a base from which they threatened both Beijing and Shanghai. The Niens began as a loose alliance of peasant militias, salt smugglers and tax protesters who evolved a highly mobile mounted army whose speed and skilful tactics confounded the government's best efforts to deal with it.

As in the Opium War, neither the *Banners* nor the militias raised by local gentry proved able to deal with these rebellions. 'The rebels travel like rats and the soldiers like cows', ran popular wisdom. 'You cannot use cows to catch rats.' Therefore, successful military resistance was the product of local initiatives, a process which ultimately contributed to the disintegration of the Ch'ing dynasty and the rise of warlordism in China. Tseng Kuo-fan, a senior bureaucrat, organized a force that became known as the Hunan army. This attempt at military modernization began as an amalgamation of mercenary bands and militias, and evolved into a relatively sophisticated force of 132,000 men organized into regiments, divisions, and corps, united by a clear chain of command. The basic structure of the Hunan army was a battalion of 650 well-paid men, competently trained, administered and supplied. Commanders recruited

Charles 'Chinese' Gordon was one of the most celebrated soldiers of fortune in China. He helped to organize the 'Ever Victorious Army' to oppose the Taiping rebellion. However, Gordon's force was disbanded in 1864 after he opposed the custom of executing prisoners of war.

their own soldiers, and were personally responsible for their performance. The purpose of these personal links was to filter out the secret society outlaws, heterodox religious sects (Taipings), bandits and rabble who had done so much to undermine the political loyalty, military efficiency and discipline of the militias. Tseng also sought to enlist as officers the disgruntled demi-monde of unsuccessful candidates for the imperial bureaucracy. Intelligent young men who had failed to pass the rigorous and multi-layered entrance examination often found an outlet for their ambitions among the leadership of both rebellions.

In 1862, the Hunan model was exported to Shanghai where it developed as the Anwhei army. With the help of 140 Western advisers (a group which included Charles 'Chinese' Gordon), 15,000 modern rifles, and modern artillery, some of which was eventually mounted on paddle-wheel river boats, the Anhwei army became an even more formidable force than its Hunan counterpart. Though each army was instrumental in crushing the internal revolts, and was recognized as indispensable, especially after the *Banners* were destroyed in 1860, neither was destined to survive. Traditionalists decried foreign influence, especially in the Anhwei army, as a humiliation. Gordon's 'Ever Victorious Army', a branch of the Anhwei force, was disbanded in 1864 after he argued with Chinese leaders over the execution of POWs. Plans to create a modern Chinese navy were put on hold because it would rely too much on foreigners. Expense was also an issue. China was simply too inward-looking, too culturally aloof, and too financially destitute, to adapt effectively to the Western challenge.

DECISIVE VICTORY VERSUS ATTRITION STRATEGIES

Decisive military engagements were rare in colonial combat. Prolonged periods of irregular warfare, sequences of indecisive skirmishes, might follow even the most ostensibly impressive battlefield victory. In these conditions, even the best commanders fell back on attrition strategies to bring the enemy to heel, but only at the price of incredible hardship. Amerindians were worn down by disease and starvation as colonists burned their corn, destroyed food caches, drove off their game and kept them from fishing spots. Without powder and ammunition, their villages were destroyed by colonial expeditions, guided by Amerindian scouts.

In India, Wellesley burned food and crops and threatened to hang merchants who supplied food to insurgents fighting on amidst the debris of Tipu's empire. Callwell maintained that the trump card of the British in India was that they could always identify and destroy any village that challenged British rule. The guerrilla war between royalist and independence factions in what is modern-day Bolivia was especially vicious, with Amerindians on both sides willing to burn villages and attack missions.

In Algeria, Bugeaud raised the razzia, or raid, to a strategic concept as his troops destroyed crops, rounded up livestock, and burned villages on the theory that if the Algerians could not eat, they could not fight.

General Aleksei Ermolov, a hero of the Napoleonic Wars and governor general of Georgia and the Caucasus, adopted a lines or siege approach to the resistance in the Caucasus – expeditions moved forward to seize important positions, which were then fortified as bases for economic warfare, and worse, against the population. Ermolov justified his harsh pacification policy: 'One execution saves hundreds of

Russians from destruction and thousands of Muslims from treason.' In the eastern Caucasus, the Russians systematically cut down forests and denied grazing land to insurgents. In the western Caucasus, a scorched-earth policy combined with simple eviction forced the migration of the Cherkes population, followed by resettlement of the area with Cossacks and Russians. The Russian General M. D. Skobelev held to the principle that 'in Asia, the harder you hit them, the longer they will remain quiet afterwards', a philosophy espoused by those fighting the Amerindians who believed extermination and deportation to be the optimum way to deal with savages.

This type of economic warfare caused difficulties not only on the ground but also at home. In the colonies, it served to point up the dilemma that was to bedevil Western soldiers until the end of the twentieth century – how to distinguish friend from foe. Resistance to European rule was very seldom absolute, but involved an extremely complex reaction in which political, religious, regional, ethnic, tribal and family loyalties all played a role. The safest solution from a Western perspective was simply to treat all natives as enemies until there was proof that they were otherwise.

Bugeaud saw no need to appease his opponents, arguing that only through the hard hand of war would they accept the yoke of conquest. For Bugeaud, Arab hostility was unalterable, and therefore they had to be crushed to be controlled. But even practitioners of harsh methods like Bugeaud acknowledged that they created much bad blood, and made later reconciliation of the conquered people to colonial rule very difficult. Callwell recommended that colonial commanders with an eye on making friends with the enemy afterwards attempt to overawe rather than aggravate them. He commended Hoche's methods in the Vendée, a happy combination of clemency with firmness. 'The enemy should be chastised up to a certain point, but should not be driven to desperation.' But he nevertheless conceded that 'a spirit of leniency that diminished the spirit of rebellion among French peasants could not be applied to uncivilized races (that) attribute leniency to timidity. In small wars, one is sometimes forced into committing havoc that the laws of regular warfare do not sanction.'

One risk of such a harsh approach was that, as Callwell suggested, it exasperated the enemy, thus escalating the conflict. This was certainly the case in the Caucasus, where Russian brutality pushed the mountaineers into the arms of Shamil and the Sufi order. It might also invite defeat. The Hessian Johann Ewald discovered his own inability to distinguish rebel from loyalist in the American revolution. Yet he recommended that, in any case, 'one make friends in the middle of enemy country', to avoid the revenge of the locals. As European reprisals tended to fall on natives close at hand, rather than on the guilty, indigenous peoples tended to flee when imperial troops appeared on the horizon, which naturally led the Europeans to the conclusion that deserted villages meant war.

The 1860s closed an era of imperial expansion. The economic underpinnings of the old mercantilist empires of the seventeenth and eighteenth centuries had collapsed in an era of free trade. The industrial and trade revolutions which spread from Britain to the European and North American continents mocked the idea that a nation's army must control a piece of land, or its navy rule the seas, for that nation to profit from it. The costs of both conquest and subsequent infrastructure development gobbled up any potential profits, as the French had learned in Algeria and the British in India. Businessmen like Mattheson and Jardine had pioneered the judicious use of military force to compel even a huge country like China to trade on terms favourable to outsiders. Yet, in the 1860s, the world stood on the threshold of a new era of imperial expansion fuelled by two new developments, one that gave Europe the motivation, the second that gave it the means. The first was national rivalries that encouraged nations to conquer territory, not for profit, but for prestige. The second development was the quickening pace of technology – modern weapons, transport, improved sanitary and logistical capabilities – which, it was hoped, would make imperial conquest hardly more than a stroll beneath a tropical sun.

CHAPTER THREE

Small Expeditions of Mounted Men: The High Renaissance of Imperialism

Maxim gun and carriage

Hiram Maxim, a native of Maine, invented the first machine gun in 1884. A significant improvement over the French mitrailleuse *and the unreliable Gatling, the Maxim became a standard feature of colonial military inventories by the turn of the century. As this picture of the Rifle Brigade in training suggests, however, the Maxim presented some of the same mobility problems as did artillery.*

Small Expeditions of Mounted Men: The High Renaissance of Imperialism

T HE 'HIGH RENAISSANCE' of imperialism kicked off in the 1870s and lasted until about 1905, a period during which Britain, France, the United States and Russia, and to a lesser extent Portugal, Germany and Japan, collected the corners of virtually every continent and island still up for grabs. It is no accident that imperial expansion hit its stride at the very moment when nationalism was at its apogee, for the former was an articulation of the latter. In Europe, the Wars of German Unification (1864–71) upset the balance of power and set the major loser, France, on an aggressive search for compensation abroad for her diminished status at home. In north and sub-Saharan Africa and in the Far East, France rattled the complacency of Britain, the grande dame of imperialism, whose fleet and extensive trade network had guaranteed her unrivalled access to foreign markets since Wellington sent Napoleon packing at Waterloo in 1815. Germany entered the imperial race in 1884 when Bismarck staked claims on what is now Namibia, Togo and Tanzania. A conference called at Berlin in the winter of 1884–5 to establish ground rules for this imperial land grab made matters worse, not better. Military imperialism, a staple of colonial expansion at least since Cortés, was sanctified, expanded and institutionalized. Effective occupation as the validation for colonial claims set off what French prime minister Jules Ferry called a

AFRICA c. 1875

In 1875, European colonization of Africa was hardly more advanced than it had been two hundred years earlier. There were precious few economic incentives to push inland in earlier eras when traders could purchase slaves, gold and ivory from chiefs on the coast. With the death of the slave trade, by the mid nineteenth century virtually the only African cash export was palm oil. European rivalries following the Franco-Prussian War of 1870–71, rather than a quest for riches, touched off a land rush to stake claims on the African heartland that preoccupied the century's last quarter.

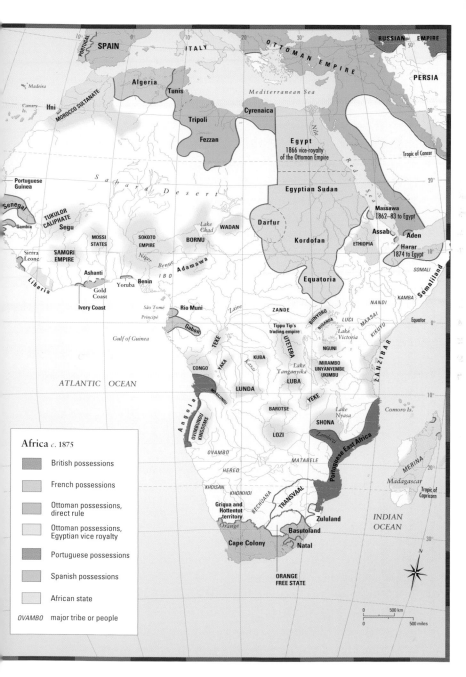

Africa c. 1875

- British possessions
- French possessions
- Ottoman possessions, direct rule
- Ottoman possessions, Egyptian vice royalty
- Portuguese possessions
- Spanish possessions
- African state

OVAMBO major tribe or people

PORTUGAL
SPAIN
ITALY
OTTOMAN EMPIRE
RUSSIAN EMPIRE
PERSIA

Madeira

Canary Is.

Ifni
MOROCCO SULTANATE

Algeria
Tunis

Mediterranean Sea

Tripoli
Fezzan
Cyrenaica

Egypt
1866 vice-royalty
of the Ottoman Empire

Nile

Tropic of Cancer

Sahara Desert

Portuguese Guinea

Egyptian Sudan

Massawa
1862–83 to Egypt

Red Sea

Senegal
TUKULOR CALIPHATE
Segu
Gambia

Lake Chad
WADAN

Darfur

Kordofan

Assab
Aden
Harar
1874 to Egypt

MOSSI STATES
SOKOTO EMPIRE
BORNU
ETHIOPIA

SOMALI

Sierra Leone
SAMORI EMPIRE

Niger
Benue
Adamawa

Ashanti
Yoruba
Benin
I B O

Liberia
Gold Coast
Ivory Coast

São Tomé
Príncipe

Rio Muni
Gabon

Equatoria

Zaire
ZANDE
Tippu Tip's trading empire
UTETERA

BUNYORO
BUGANDA
LUCI

NANDI
KAMBA
Somaliland

Gulf of Guinea

TEKE
YAKA
KUBA
Kasai

NGUNI
MIRAMBO UNYANYEMBE UKIMBU

Lake Victoria
MAASAI
KIKUYU

ZANZIBAR

Equator

CONGO
Kwa/Lundu
LUNDA

LUBA
Lake Tanganyika

YEKE

Comoro Is.

ATLANTIC OCEAN

Angola

OVIMBUNDU KINGDOMS

BAROTSE
SHONA
LOZI
Zambezi

Lake Nyasa

Portuguese East Africa

MERINA

OVAMBO

HERERO

Orange

MATABELE

Madagascar

Tropic of Capricorn

KHOISAN
KHOIKHOI

BECHUANA
TRANSVAAL

INDIAN OCEAN

Griqua and Hottentot territory
Orange

Basutoland
Zululand

Cape Colony
Natal

ORANGE FREE STATE

0   500 km
0   500 miles

'steeplechase to the unknown', as imperial soldiers rushed to explore, conquer and claim areas where earlier only the most curious, intrepid or foolhardy whites had dared venture.

The Civil War behind it, the United States was free to continue its continental expansion, and took to the sea in the aftermath of the Spanish–American war of 1898. Russia pushed into Central Asia and along the Amur river toward Manchuria. The implosion of China induced by the bullying and humiliation of unequal treaties signed at the points of foreign bayonets, energized Meiji Japan into a programme of military modernization and imperial expansion lest it, too, suffer Beijing's fate.

The altered political context of imperial expansion did not immediately transform the situation on the ground. As in the earlier period, imperial expeditions remained campaigns against nature, tests of physical endurance in which fatigue and disease claimed a greater mortality than did bullets. Imperial soldiers still struggled to impart mobility and offensive punch into their operations, to make campaigns more decisive and lessen the requirements for debilitating attrition strategies. Colonel C. E. Callwell preached the virtues of small expeditions of mounted men as the best formula for decision. The most brilliant exploits, he believed, were carried out by mounted troops alone. 'Savages, Asiatics and adversaries of that character have a great dread of the mounted man.' Callwell attributed the British difficulties in the early stages of the Indian Mutiny, and their defeat in the First South African War of 1881, to the absence of cavalry. That cavalry formed an important component of imperial expeditions cannot be denied. Horses, mules or camels supplied mobility, vital for scouting, surprise, and maintaining contact with a rapidly retreating enemy. For instance, mounted Philippine scouts and cavalry (*macabebes*) allowed US forces the advantage of mobility and surprise over Luzon at the turn of the century. But the contribution of cavalry to victory in imperial expeditions must not be exaggerated. Even Callwell confessed that mounted troops alone were not invariably a formula for success. Not all terrain was favourable to

Major General Nelson Miles, a hero of the American Civil War who had been awarded the Medal of Honor at Chancellorsville, also proved to be one of America's most tenacious Amerindian fighters, leading campaigns against the Nez Piercé in 1877 and Geronimo in 1886.

cavalry; it might be too forested, too dry, or too mountainous. Horses were too expensive and too fragile to be anything but an auxiliary commodity on most expeditions, which is why most commanders in the early nineteenth century, and many who came after, relied principally on infantry. And even in conditions where mounted soldiers were the arm of choice, as in the American west where horse soldiers were most likely to close with the enemy, horses tired quickly and, after a week, the cavalry might be less mobile and have less firepower than the infantry.

Cavalry was most effective when it co-operated with artillery and infantry. However, in conditions of imperial warfare, cavalry commanders might be tempted to operate on their own, thus exposing their forces to unnecessary risks. George Armstrong Custer's demise on the Little Bighorn in 1876 offers the most dramatic and celebrated example of a mounted man's inclination to ride off over the horizon away from infantry support and get into trouble. It is significant and ironic that General Nelson A. Miles's relentless, and ultimately successful, pursuit of Sitting Bull to avenge Custer's defeat was carried out mainly with infantry. It was precisely to correct the problem of cavalry operating without infantry support that the French General François de Négrier created mule-mounted infantry companies in 1881, whose purpose was to provide long-range support for cavalry operating in the Sud-Oranais of Algeria. Like the cavalry in the American Civil War and in the campaigns in the American West, these companies learned to fight dismounted after a company of the Foreign Legion was destroyed trying to fight on mule-back at the Chott Tigri in the Sud-Oranais of Algeria in April 1882. These mule-mounted companies remained a feature of Foreign Legion units in North Africa until the Second World War.

The Second South African (Boer) War is regarded as the quintessential cavalry war, and in many respects it was, at least in its final stages. But it is useful to remember that the firepower of Boer Mausers during the opening phase of the conflict forced the British cavalry to fight dismounted. As the war slipped into its guerrilla phase, British cavalry never matched that of the Boer raiders in mobility. Ultimately, the British cavalry became an element in an attrition strategy which saw it organized into extended lines to drive Boer guerrillas against fixed lines of barbed wire and blockhouses. And even then, what these cavalry drives succeeded in doing was to force the Boers to abandon their cumbersome

Mounted Boer fighters dominated the latter phase of the Second South African War. They acquired a mobility that the British found impossible to match until, taking a leaf from Bugeaud's book, they simply removed anything or anyone who might supply the insurgents with a means to resist.

Blockhouses, like this one used in South Africa,
were a variant of the 'lines' approach used by the
Russians in the Caucasus and the Spanish in
Morocco. In South Africa, blockhouses connected
by barbed wire, rail lines in some cases, and
searchlights formed lines against which sweeps
of British cavalry would attempt to drive elusive
Boer fighters.

wagons, livestock and dismounted soldiers, ultimately reducing them to starvation. Finally, mobility cut both ways. In South-West Africa, Hendrik Witbooi forced Captain Curt von François to come to terms in 1893 after the Nama leader had captured virtually all the horses around Windhoek in a series of daring raids, thus making German pursuit impossible. Horses raised on the South African veld, more robust than the mounts imported by the British, gave the Boers a decided edge in mobility in the South African War. Likewise, the French in Algeria were never able to match in mobility raiders out of Morocco or camel-mounted Tuareg in the Sahara.

Callwell's purpose was not to extend the natural life of an antiquated if noble arm out of sheer nostalgia. What Callwell, indeed all colonial commanders, sought was mobility. 'The problem is not to move faster,' General de Négrier wrote of North African warfare, 'but to go further, for longer. Fire fights are rare here. We fight with volleys of kilometres. You have to march.' One of de Négrier's successors in the Sud-Oranais, General Hubert Lyautey, was fond of repeating that, in Africa, one defends oneself by moving. 'From the days of Clive down to the present time,' insisted Callwell, 'victory has been achieved by vigor and dash rather than by force of numbers.' One major advantage of this approach was political – home governments eager for results favoured a one-blow approach over more patient strategies which lengthened conflicts and raised the costs, both financial and political.

As suggested in the previous chapter, the impediments to rapid victory against an often elusive foe across country which was usually remote and invariably inhospitable were immense. Disease was one. Until quinine became available in a distilled form in the 1840s, armies in the Caribbean and West Africa wasted away from falciparum malaria carried by the anopheline mosquito. The *Aedes aegypti* mosquito, endemic to urban areas and military camps, hollowed out whole expeditions with yellow fever, which consigned 75 per cent of its victims to delirium, coma and death. Because white troops perished at a much higher rate from these and other endemic diseases, commanders preferred to recruit a high percentage of native soldiers for their expeditions.

Logistics were the Achilles' heel of any imperial expedition. The task of accumulating supplies, not to mention pack animals, in remote areas was a long and arduous one, which contributed to the expense of a campaign, a condition which invited opposition, both political and military. Horses were fragile commodities, and a commander might court disaster if he relied too heavily on them for the success of an expedition. For instance, the longevity of the Seminole uprising relied in part on the fact that the small American force sent to master it in the summer of 1836 lost 600 horses to sickness. As has been noted, in his 1845 expedition in the Caucasus, General Vorontsov had to spike his guns because 400 of the 635 horses used to draw them had perished.

The problem for the commander was how to balance the numbers required for security and success with the constraints of logistics. From an operational perspective, expeditions that were too large might have their hands full simply sustaining themselves on the coast, much less be able to push inland. This was initially the case in 1868 when 10,000 British troops in Abyssinia required 26,000 pack animals and 12,000 followers to lumber inland. In 1894, French planners estimated that 18,000 to 20,000 porters and mule drivers would be required to support a 12,000-man expeditionary force to Madagascar. The inclusion of the two-wheeled metal *voiture Lefèvre* allowed the number of porters to be reduced to 7,000 when the French invaded the following year. But the expedition stalled on the coast as roads and bridges over which the vehicles (called *la fièvre*, or 'fever wagon' by the troops) could pass had to be constructed. General Charles Duchesne, his force perishing from disease before even a shot could be fired, was forced to cut loose from his logistics and march on Tananarive with a light column of 1,500 men. The French requisitioned 35,000 camels to supply the Tuat expedition of 1901–2, of which 25,000 perished at the hands of French troops inexperienced in the finer points of camel handling. As a consequence, the economy of southern Algeria was devastated and took years to recover. 'I do not think that there has been a massacre comparable to that of 1901,' the Sahara expert E. F. Gautier wrote. 'The jackals and the vultures along the way were overwhelmed with the immensity of their task.' The German governor of South-West Africa complained in 1894 that the country was so deficient in water and pasture land that a force of 100 men would pose an almost insoluble supply problem. 'We would be defeated not by the people, but by Nature.' In 1896, he actually

The 1895 French invasion of Madagascar nearly came to grief when General Duchesne lingered for too long in the island's malarial lowlands to construct roads and bridges to support a thrust toward Tananarive. His force melting away from disease, Duchesne was obliged to strike inland with a 1,500-man 'flying column'.

returned almost a quarter of his force to Germany because he lacked the horses and oxen to support a force larger than seven hundred men.

Logistical difficulties, which constrained strategic mobility, could be eased in two ways: the first was, as in the past, to advance along water routes. The Niger and Congo river networks offered multiple routes of entry into sub-Saharan Africa, first for explorers, and then for expeditions of armed men. The entire French strategy for the penetration of the western Sudan was to construct posts along the Senegal and eventually the Niger rivers. The strategy of those who opposed them, then, had to be to block those rivers. When, in 1857,

In the colonies, rivers often offered the most obvious routes of advance. The 1892 French invasion of Dahomey was greatly facilitated by the gunboat Topaz, *which shadowed the French advance along the Ouémé river and helped to shatter several Dahomian attacks.*

al-Hajj Umar threw 20,000 Tokolor *sofas* (warriors) against the French post at Medine, General Louis Faidherbe crammed 500 soldiers with artillery on two steamships at St-Louis de Senegal and, in ten days, sailed 400 miles up the Senegal river to relieve the siege. The fabled city of Timbuktu fell to a French river flotilla in January 1894. It is no accident that the intrepid band of Frenchmen led by Colonel Marchand, who left the mouth of the Congo in 1896 to appear, almost two years later, on the upper Nile at a place called Fashoda, transported a disassembled steamboat during the overland part of their trek. Nor is it any wonder that, when General Kitchener moved south from Khartoum to challenge them in 1898, he came by steamboat. The French tried to penetrate Cochin-China on the Mekong river in the 1860s because they believed it offered a path into southern China. When that failed, they tried the Red and Clear rivers into Tonkin two decades later. When General Négrier abandoned the Red river network to advance overland to Lang Son on the Chinese border in 1885, he outran his logistics and got into trouble. General Dodds followed the Ouémé river to invade Dahomey in 1892.

However, the decision to advance along a water line was not invariably a happy one. For instance, the decision by French planners in Paris to land at Manjunga on the Madagascar Channel and advance on Tananarive along the Betsiboka/Ikopa rivers rather than choose a shorter overland route from the port of Vatomandry on Madagascar's east coast, nearly sunk the expedition. A hidden coral reef off Manjunga complicated the off-loading of the ships, the ocean swells on the Betsiboka estuary swamped many river craft, while the rivers, although unnavigable very far inland, proved to be rich in malarial mosquitoes. The Pearl, Yellow and Yangtze rivers offered Western gunboats access to the Chinese heartland, while Russian gunboats approached from the north along the Amur.

Railways offered a second method of resolving logistical difficulties. The British imported their own locomotives, cars and track in 1868 for the invasion of Abyssinia. Railways determined many of the lines of advance chosen by British forces in the Boer War and linked the blockhouse system built by Kitchener in the later phase of the war. However, railways had several drawbacks from a military viewpoint. The first was that they were not plentiful in the undeveloped world, and the effort expended to build them across desolate or malarial countryside diverted military assets and desperately increased the costs of a campaign. In the western Sudan, attempts to construct a railway in the 1880s to support the French advance from Senegal to the Niger river became an expensive farce which spiked the costs of the military campaign, invited parliamentary scrutiny of the army's financial mismanagement and contributed nothing to the security of French posts. A second problem was that although railways could bring troops and supplies to the railhead, the effort to shift *matériel* beyond that point was immense. Third, unlike western Europe where a profligate rail network offered commanders strategic mobility, the paucity of rail

Railways offered one solution to logistical problems. However, railroads had their drawbacks, all of which were obvious in the Boer War: they made for very predictable lines of advance that might be blocked; they required significant manpower to build and maintain; they were vulnerable to attack; finally, the enemy learned to concentrate far away from the railheads.

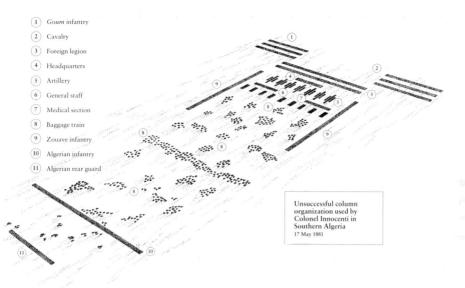

1. *Goum* infantry
2. Cavalry
3. Foreign legion
4. Headquarters
5. Artillery
6. General staff
7. Medical section
8. Baggage train
9. Zouave infantry
10. Algerian infantry
11. Algerian rear guard

Unsuccessful column
organization used by
Colonel Innocenti in
Southern Algeria
17 May 1881

In May 1881, Bou Amama successfully attacked the Innocenti column at Moualok
in southern Algeria by enticing the armed elements forward to break an obvious
ambush, and then falling upon the lightly protected convoy. Colonel (later General)
François de Négrier subsequently reorganized his convoy defence as a 'mobile
echelon' of mule-mounted Foreign Legionnaires and artillery that could swing to
defend against attack from any direction, while permitting the column a more
flexible marching formation over irregular terrain. Négrier also dispensed with his
goums – irregular tribal levies – whose resemblance to the enemy confused the
Innocenti column and caused them to hold fire until too late.

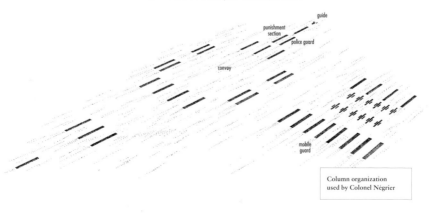

Column organization
used by Colonel Négrier

lines abroad limited strategic options. British advances along rail lines in the early months of the Boer War were so predictable that Boers simply had to fortify obvious choke points and wait for the British to attack. In South-West Africa, the Herero learned to concentrate far away from the rail lines and force the Germans to come to them, thereby amplifying the logistical burden for their enemies.

When the push into the hinterland began, supply trains slowed the column to a snail's pace, and offered a vulnerable target. This circumscribed the offensive capacities of expeditions forced to employ a disproportionate number of troops and artillery to defend supply trains from hostile attack. For this reason, imperial expeditions were often categorized as campaigns against nature. As in Wellesley's day, no imperial commander could hope for success until he had solved his logistical problems.

Unlike Wellesley, however, soldiers in the late nineteenth century could turn to technology to help them solve their operational and logistical problems. However, the impact of technology on imperial warfare, indeed on all warfare, has frequently been misunderstood. Not only was the change a slow one, but also technology was more important to the logistical tail than at the sharp end of imperial expeditions. On the surface, at least, the introduction of breech-loading rifles in the 1860s, and of machine guns in the 1880s, changed the equation of colonial battles. But although Hilaire Belloc could write, 'Whatever happens we have got/the Maxim gun and they have not', the truth was that firepower gave Europeans an important, but by no means a decisive, advantage. For one thing, technology, like mobility, was available to both sides. There was no shortage of merchants of death to sell modern rifles to indigenous peoples; it is reckoned that

MAXIM GUN AND CARRIAGE

over 16 million firearms were imported by Africans in the course of the nineteenth century. Colonial officials, eager to introduce a fatal touch of chaos to African empires which dwelt in conditions of scarcely stifled unrest, might supply weapons to minor chieftains or pretenders to thrones as a means of undermining the position of a local ruler. European rivalries also played a role in arming indigenous resistance – the governor of French Somaliland supplied Menelik with a gift of 100,000 rifles and 2 million tons of ammunition after Britain backed Italy's assertion of a protectorate over Ethiopia in 1891, rifles used to good effect against the Italians five years later at Adowa. The Italians also contributed to the arms transfer in North Africa when they abandoned 5,000 rifles and crates of ammunition in a headlong flight back to Tripoli in the face of Sanusi opposition in 1915. Although it may safely be consigned to the 'sore loser' category, survivors of the Little Bighorn alleged that Sitting Bull had shot them off the field with Winchester repeaters, while their ability to reply was muted by single-shot Springfields. These complaints are identical to those of French soldiers in Tonkin in 1885 about their single-shot 1874-model Gras rifles with which they faced Chinese troops armed with repeaters. The French discovered that both the Dahomians in 1892 and the Malagasies in 1895 possessed modern rifles, although they used them badly when they used them at all. It was reckoned that in 1890–91 alone, the Herero traded almost 20,000 cattle for weapons and ammunition in South-West Africa. Nevertheless, when rebellion against the Germans erupted in 1904, fewer than one-third of the warriors were armed with rifles. It is also likely that the superior weaponry of the imperial invaders convinced many native chiefs that co-operation, rather than confrontation, offered the most prudent strategy. The accuracy of Boer Mausers caused the British to alter their tactics in the Second South African War of 1899–1902, as well as to cease the use of expanding dum-dum rounds (named after the arms factory in India), so effective against the Mahdi's forces at Omdurman in 1898, as unsuitable to a white man's war.

The advent of machine guns did give Europeans firepower advantages in defensive situations. It appears that the Russians and Americans were the first to add them to the inventories of armed expeditions in Central Asia and the American West. However, their general use in imperial warfare was impeded by both technical and tactical factors. Early versions like the *mitrailleuse* and the Gatling were heavy and unreliable. Most commanders realized that a weapon which jammed at critical moments posed a distinct danger, which was why Custer left his Gatling behind when he departed for the Little Bighorn. Chelmsford carried them into action against the Zulus in 1879, but the Africans learned to work around them and attack on the flank. So firepower did not save him at Isandlwana. Conventional wisdom in the early days also assigned these weapons to the artillery to be used in batteries, rather than distributed to infantry and cavalry units.

Despite the appearance of the Maxim, this Gatling, though obsolete and unreliable, defends a laager in Bulawayo in 1896. Machine guns worked to their maximum advantage during the Matabele War because the enemy massed in great numbers to attack laagers.

The lighter, more reliable Maxim gun began to appear on colonial battlefields in the 1890s, to be used by the British on the North-West Frontier, and to best effect in the Matabele War of 1896, when armed police of the Chartered Company and volunteers simply laagered their wagons and mowed down the Africans, who charged with reckless courage. But Maxim guns were seldom a battle winner, for at least two reasons. First, they were not well suited for warfare in mountains or jungles where the enemy fought dispersed or was invisible. Pushed too far forward, they might become isolated and their crews overwhelmed. Second, they remained too few to decide the outcome of a campaign – the British possessed only six Maxims at Omdurman. Maxims were not free of mechanical problems, as the French discovered during the Moroccan attack at Menabba in eastern Morocco in April 1908, when sand jammed the mechanisms of their machine guns. During the Boer War of 1899–1902, the Transvaal government equipped its troops with a number of Maxims, which they regarded as a cheap and efficient form of light artillery, while the British included them in their flying columns. But it was only the Russo-Japanese War of 1904–5 which revealed the value of large numbers of machine-guns, and their tactical use on the offensive as well as the defensive. And even then, the machine gun remained a relatively scarce item in military inventories well into the First World War.

The remoteness of colonial battlefields continued to make artillery a problem. Light mountain guns carried on the backs of mules or camels and able to be assembled quickly were available from the 1840s, but they did not pack much of a wallop. In areas where pack animals were scarce, artillery might be disassembled and carried by porters. But it was burdensome, forfeited surprise, and was more trouble that it was worth. Artillery might be useful against forts, walled villages, or defensive enclosures. But after taking high casualties in frontal assaults, the French in Tonkin, like the British who stormed Maori *pahs* in New Zealand, discovered that dynamite or, better still, a manoeuvre against the line of retreat was usually sufficient to induce a precipitate

The Battle of Isandlwana

Dramatic defeats of imperial armies by indigenous forces were relatively rare in the imperial era, but not unknown. Zulu Impis attacked in a 'cow horns' formation fairly typical of the more sophisticated indigenous African armies. While this strategy, developed for raiding, usually failed against well-disciplined imperial forces, the attackers here saturated a defence strung out on too vast a perimeter.

Battle of Isandlwana
22 January 1879

---

1 British column camps at Isandlwana. At daybreak on the 22 January, Lord Chelmsford sends out a column to intercept a Zulu force, leaving some 800 troops and 400 native levies to guard the camp

2 Midday, the Zulu attack develops with the main force rapidly approaching hastily founded British positions

3 Col. Durnford retreats and takes position on the right flank next to Bradstreets company

4 The Zulu army, some 10,000 strong, closes on the British positions, and overwhelms the British line. Only a small number manage to escape the final onslaught

Isandlwana — Mkwen

uNokhenke — uKhandempemvu

YOUNGHUSBAND   NNC   ZIKHALIS HORSE   MOSTYN

iDududu, iMbube, iSangqu

Wagon Parks

Wagon Parks

Wagon Parks

Wagon Parks

Mahlabamkhosi

Modern firepower was usually sufficient to withstand frontal assaults by poorly armed natives. However, despite their significant firepower advantage, Chelmsford's troops were overwhelmed in part because the Natal Kaffirs, who had been confided a critical portion of the defence line, were inadequately armed and disciplined.

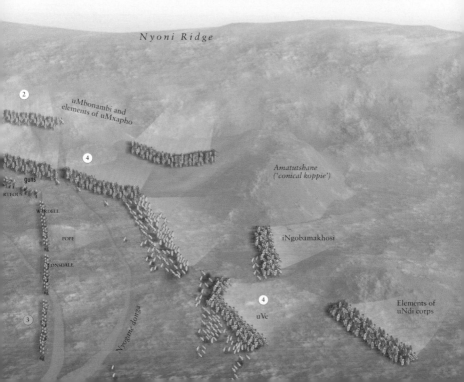

Nyoni Ridge

uMbonambi and elements of uMxapho

guns

RTEOUS

WARDELL

POPE

LONSDALE

Nyogani donga

uVe

Amatutshane ('conical koppie')

iNgobamakhosi

Elements of uNdi corps

evacuation. In any case, it came almost as a relief if the enemy chose to fight from these defensive positions because it lessened the threat of ambushes or surprise attacks, which the European soldiers, especially those fighting in dense jungle, feared most.

In the last quarter of the nineteenth century, small artillery pieces like the Hotchkiss became part of the inventories of expeditionary forces. Larger guns, like Creusot 75s, might be used extensively, especially if the battlefield was not too remote, and the enemy showed a preference for massing to attack, as did Samori's *sofas*, the Dahomians in 1892, or the Moroccans at Sidi-Bou Othman, outside Marrakesh, in September 1912. Native fortifications were easily smashed by artillery, which also allowed Europeans to break Boxer resistance at Peking (Beijing) in 1900. Those fighting on the defensive might also be vulnerable. The British scurried to add heavy artillery to their arsenals during the Boer War. Naval artillery mounted on gunboats supported land operations in Tonkin, on the Niger, against the Dahomians, on the Nile and, of course, in China. However, the effect of artillery on the enemy, especially on dispersed, irregular forces, was more psychological than physical. At Isandlwana, Zulus threw themselves to the ground each time the gunners sprang back prior to pulling the lanyards, so that shells from the camp's two artillery pieces screamed harmlessly overhead. Artillery was used to dissuade Herero tribesmen from attacking German settlements at the beginning of the rebellions of 1904. German General Lothar von Trotha also employed artillery in the offensive phase of operations when he brought thirty guns and twelve Maxims against Herero tribesmen at Waterberg on 11–12 August, 1904. Although German firepower inflicted few casualties, von Trotha succeeded in his true purpose, which was to drive the Herero into the Omaheke Desert where hundreds perished of thirst. The French found that shrapnel had little effect on Moroccans, who sought refuge in palm groves or behind walls of *ksour* (fortified villages). However, when in September 1908 a Moroccan *harka* concentrated against eighteen guns of a French column before Bou

Denib in eastern Morocco, the result was a massacre. But it was always hard to predict the proper mix of shrapnel and impact shells to be carried on campaign.

Indigenous peoples usually had little success when they attempted to adopt artillery. The premise of China's 'Self-Strengthening Movement', spurred by the 1861 occupation of Beijing by an Anglo-French expeditionary force, was that, since Western superiority was based on technology, the adoption of technology would bring strength. Unfortunately for the reformers, the hold of tradition was such that they found it difficult to adjust their institutions to accommodate technology. The fact that the Chinese had to rely on foreigners to train them in the use of artillery made that weapon automatically suspect in the eyes of traditionalists. Modernity also came at a price that was higher than China could afford. Chinese armies were basically infantry armies, and commanders who possessed artillery tended to treat it as a status symbol to be preserved as a totem of modernity, rather than integrated into an effective tactical system. The Chinese used artillery against the French in Tonkin in 1885, although only late in the

Alexandria in 1882 after bombardment by the British fleet in response to a nationalist uprising in Egypt. Naval artillery was regularly mustered to intimidate foreign potentates to give in to imperial demands or to quell rebellion.

campaign did it begin to prove its effectiveness. French and Russian advisers were said to have supervised the crews of Emperor Menelik's mountain guns at Adowa in 1896. Moroccan troops opposing the French in western Morocco after the turn of the century occasionally enticed a non-lethal blast from one of their antique guns. These pieces might be important, even decisive, in conflicts among native groups. Four artillery pieces captured in skirmishes with the French allowed al-Hajj Umar Tal to extend the Tokolor empire on the southern bank of the Senegal river in the 1850s, although their impact was thought to be more psychological than physical. The rise of the powerful Galoui clan in southern Morocco can be traced to a 77mm cannon taken from the sultan's army in 1893. This artillery piece allowed Madani el Galoui to bust the fortresses of his rivals who guarded the passes of the High Atlas, thus making him the power broker of Marrakesh with whom the sultan, and ultimately the French, were forced to deal. Cuban revolutionaries organized artillery units which they employed to chase Spanish troops from Bayamo in Oriente province and Victoria de las Tunas in 1897. But the Spaniards appeared little inclined to defend these small provincial towns in any case. As with small arms, even when indigenous forces counted artillery in their arsenals, they seldom had sufficient shells to affect a battle's outcome.

Firepower might be a factor in victory if the enemy obligingly tried to replicate European methods, as did the Indian mutineers in 1857, or Egyptian troops at Tel-el-Kebir in 1882. Better still, if they massed in a 'holy war' response, as at Omdurman in 1898, at Bou Denib, Morocco in 1908, or Marrakesh in 1912. But Europeans had prevailed in pitched battles like Assaye in 1803, on the Sikkak river in Algeria in 1836, or at Isly in 1844. It was superior tactics and discipline, rather than firepower, which had assured European victory in these set-piece engagements. When these elements were absent, as with ill-trained and poorly led Italian forces at Adowa in 1896, the results could be disastrous. However, European advantages in firepower, tactics, and discipline might be nullified by geography and by the enemy.

British forces crush Egyptian nationalists at Tel-el-Kebir in 1882. The British imposition of supervisory officials on the khedive (viceroy) in 1881 to protect the Suez Canal angered both Egyptian nationalists, as well as the French, who retaliated in 1898 by staking a claim to the Egyptian Sudan at Fashoda.

The turning point for Europeans came in the 1860s and 1870s, when firepower and organizational ability allied with technology to give the Europeans the advantage. While innovative commanders like Wellesley or Bugeaud always attempted to organize expeditions efficiently within the confines of pre-industrial capabilities, the decisive development came, perhaps, with the Abyssinian expedition of 1868, when the British imported an entire railway to support the advance into the interior. However, it was General Sir Garnet Wolseley who probably first achieved the marriage of technology and organization during the Ashanti campaign of 1873–4. To be sure, Wolseley defeated the Ashanti in battle thanks to Snider rifles and 7-pounder guns. But the battle was almost incidental to the success of the campaign, which had been a triumph of administrative planning. In future, successful commanders, like French General Dodds in Dahomey (1892), would imitate Wolseley by reducing the size of expeditions to around 3,500 men, and take care to provide roads, way stations, porterage, pack animals, tinned food (which increasingly replaced dry provisions like macaroni or rice which required water to cook), potable water, and quinine for their troops, all of which would ensure a maximum number of rifles on line and a rapid conclusion of a campaign.

Admittedly, this lesson was unevenly applied, in part because, although the Ashanti campaign proved a marvel of technical organization, its success relied largely on the fact that it was a punitive expedition, not a campaign of conquest. Because Wolseley rapidly withdrew his force after destroying the Ashanti capital, the campaign was barren of strategic results. Other commanders seeking more permanent outcomes were obliged to resort to large expeditions. Russian expeditions in Central Asia were essentially expeditions cast into the desert to lay siege to fortified towns, and required what, in effect, were small armies. In Indo-China in 1884–5 the French required a considerable force to take on a Chinese army allied with local Black Flag resistance. Logistics remained the weak spot of all of these operations. When the enemy force was smaller, or fragmented, then successful commanders could resolve the dilemma of how to combine mobility with a force sufficiently large to defend itself by reducing their baggage to a minimum. General George Crook's 1883 Sierra Madre campaign against Geronimo was considered a model: a small, aggressively led force was guided by Apache auxiliaries with supplies carried on mule back. Flying columns were most effective against fixed positions like a village in places where the enemy was too few to take advantage of their frailties – Burma, Tonkin in the 1890s, Rhodesia, and against Boer commandos in the latter part of the Second South African War. General Lothar von Trotha so arranged his converging columns at Waterberg as to offer the Herero the choice between immediate death in the teeth of his superior firepower, or slow extinction in the sandveld of the Omaheke. Most chose the latter.

Flying columns had their drawbacks, however. Co-ordinating the arrival of these columns from different directions on a single, often elusive, objective was a difficult task in the era before radio communications. Lyautey complained that ambitious officers in charge of one prong of converging columns in Tonkin often sabotaged operations by attempting to be the first to reach the objective, alerting the enemy and allowing him to flee before his escape route was cut off.

'Each thought only of stealing the affair from the other, each manoeuvring to escape the control of the Colonel, to pull off a *coup de main*, and then cover himself with a *fait accompli*,' he complained. As Callwell noted, the supply train could become a millstone which both slowed down a force, and disorganized it, especially in broken country, so making it vulnerable to ambush. Poor intelligence and the poisoning of wells so debilitated Hicks Pasha on the Nile in 1883 that he fell victim to a Mahdist attack. If the force were too small, it might find itself the prey rather than the stalker. This happened in Mexico between 1862 and 1867, and even in North Africa, where French columns were continually surprised and sometimes overwhelmed because they were too small to defend themselves. Similar fates befell Custer in 1876, Chelmsford in 1879, and Hicks Pasha on the Nile in 1883. For these reasons, Callwell regarded light or flying columns as only a temporary expedient or a minor operation in a larger campaign.

A colonial commander who resorted to flying columns usually did so because he confronted the most dreaded of all situations – guerrilla warfare. From a military standpoint, regular armies, even those with substantial colonial experience, were poorly equipped to deal with it. An elusive enemy could control the strategic pace of the war, withdraw deep into the country, and nullify the technological and firepower advantage which should naturally be enjoyed by the invaders. To match this, European commanders required a substantial reordering of their military system. This was never easy to do, and officers who advocated such things as light, mobile, largely locally recruited forces with logistical systems to match, were regarded as eccentrics whose innovations seldom survived their departure. A reliable intelligence network was vital for irregular warfare, a field in which traditionally-minded commanders were usually loathe to work. Nevertheless, the British continued a tradition begun by Wellesley, who put considerable effort into creating reliable intelligence networks both in India and later in the Peninsula. In North Africa, the French developed the Arab Bureaux, later renamed the *service de renseignement* (intelligence service) whose task was both to collect intelligence on the tribes, and to administer them in areas controlled by the army. Indeed, an essential element of the *tache d'huile* or 'oil spot' method of pacification pioneered by Gallieni in Tonkin and Madagascar, and later by Lyautey in eastern Algeria and Morocco, was that the creation of a market-place would draw in the tribes from whom one could glean intelligence and recruit locals to act as scouts. In the Philippines, General Frederick Funston established an intelligence network which relied principally on paying generous cash bonuses for good information, and on the carelessness of his enemies, a generally literate group who exhibited an unfortunate tendency to write everything down, including the identity of their leaders, who could then be arrested. Working on the basis of intelligence, Funston was able to organize rapid offensive operations to attack guerrilla bases and capture important rebel leaders. His most celebrated action combined intelligence and deception. Using captured documents, he identified the location of the headquarters of insurgent General Emilio Aguinaldo. Funston disguised his Philippine scouts as guerrillas and their officers as prisoners, inserted them by sea, and arrived at Aguinaldo's camp undetected to seize the general.

Some of these problems – stamina, mobility, logistics and costs – could be resolved in part by substituting locally recruited soldiers for Europeans. The British and the French evolved a formula of one European for two soldiers of imperial origins. But imperial levies were not an automatic solution, and much ink was spilled by colonial officers on their best utilization. If a commander employed irregular levies of cossacks, *goums*, or simply tribal formations armed with surplus weapons, he might discover that they were more trouble than they were worth. Part of the problem lay in a different cultural approach to warfare – indigenous levies often could not understand the European preference for frontal assaults and seizing territory or fortresses. For them, the goal of battle was seldom the extinction of the enemy. Rather, battle was primarily an exercise in personal bravery, a flirtation with danger. The pay-off was the enhancement of one's personal reputation,

Emilio Aguinaldo (seated third from right, bottom row) in 1896. The Philippine resistance was led by a European-educated Luzon élite, whose democratic, nationalist appeal enjoyed limited resonance both among a traditional peasant society and across a broad archipelago of islands.

and the collection of trophies like female slaves or livestock. African tribes, like their Amerindian counterparts, often sought to incorporate villages into their empires and economic systems, and merely saw European soldiers as a means to that end. For European soldiers, whose goals were to extend imperial authority, the utilization of native levies in their raw form under their own headmen was rather like the employment of poison gas or submarines during the First World War – they made the battlefield a very messy, disagreeable and dangerous place, but seldom proved a decisive element in combat. Native levies swarmed all over the battlefield, kicking up dust and getting in the line of fire of European troops who, soon unable to distinguish friend from foe, might come in for some nasty surprises. For instance, during the Bou-Amama revolt of 1881 in the Sud-Oranais region of Algeria, a French column lost seventy-two soldiers and most of their convoy at Chellala after Arab horsemen, whom the French believed to be part of a French-organized *goum*, were allowed to approach uncontested.

From the perspective of European commanders, indigenous levies were difficult to control both on and off the battlefield. This was in part linked to pay, or rather, the lack of it. Colonial expeditions were horribly expensive, a fact which raised opposition at home. It was in part to circumvent that opposition that commanders in the colonies struck upon the idea of recruiting soldiers locally. But indigenous troops might also give imperialism a bad press. Indian troops under British command repeatedly misbehaved during expeditions in China. Much of the devastation in western Sudan occurred because the French relied heavily on tribal levies, or poorly disciplined Senegalese or Soudannais *tirailleurs*, who were quick to abandon the firing line to snatch booty and female slaves. For instance, of 3,600 troops in the French column which captured Segou in 1890, barely fifty were European, and another 500 were regular native recruits. The rest were porters and auxiliaries furnished by African allies. Indeed, the practice of arming and leading native irregulars against other tribes led to one of the greatest scandals of French expansion in Africa, the destructive and ultimately mutinous Voulet–Chanoine expedition of 1898. The scouts and the *macabebes* (Philippine cavalry) recruited among the Ilocano population by the US Army on Luzon acquired a reputation for brutality against Tagalog prisoners and villages. Loyalty might also be an issue. The Germans used native levies extensively in South-West Africa. However, they complained of the lack of bravery among the Herero on their side as compared with those fighting for the enemy. When the Herero revolt spread to the Nama in October 1904, von Trotha immediately gave orders to disarm his Nama contingent, who were deported to Togo to keep them from joining in the rebellion. The Italian expedition against the Sanusi in Tripolitania in 1915 collapsed when many of the indigenous auxiliaries turned on Italian troops. The flight of the poorly armed Natal Kaffirs at Isandlwana left a gap some 300 yards wide in the British lines that fatally compromised the defence. Thousands of Zulus poured through to take the British companies from the rear.

Nevertheless, it is no exaggeration to say that without troops recruited in the colonies, the French and the British could neither have conquered nor garrisoned their empires. In the American West, Amerindians performed essential service as scouts – Crook's employment of Apache scouts in Arizona in 1872–3, and his use of Crows to hound Sitting Bull after Custer's defeat made the difference between success and failure. In Luzon, General Frederick Funston organized the Headquarters Scouts, which served as a scouting,

Apache scouts and trackers enlisted by the US Army to hunt Geronimo in Arizona in 1882–3. Imperial soldiers regularly enlisted native irregulars as scouts, to gather intelligence, and on occasion to serve as a strike force.

intelligence-gathering and strike force. Disguised as peasants, they surprised and destroyed insurgent roadblocks set up to collect taxes. Most of the scouts were Ilocanos, whose traditional distrust of the Tagalogs (who formed the core of the *insurrectos*) made them especially reliable.

But Crook's and Funston's experiments found few imitators. American officers, like their European counterparts, preferred to oblige native levies to conform to European standards of drill and discipline. This was in part because they never fully trusted them to perform well or faithfully in less conventional roles. Invariably, they got mixed results. While some of these units were excellent, commanders who created coloured versions of European regiments might discover that recruitment dried up, and that natives lost the rusticity, spontaneity and resilience that supplied the edge over European troops in mobile operations. To draw the best from these troops also required an officer corps knowledgeable in the languages and customs of their men, and willing on campaign to endure a standard of living that gave new meaning to the concept of misery. For instance, French officers serving with Saharan troops were not only expected to endure sandstorms, cantankerous camels and temperatures that would roast a stoker on a battleship but they were also expected to do this on a starvation diet of dates and couscous.

INDIGENOUS RESPONSE

So far, we have discussed the problems of European adaptation. How does one explain the generally inadequate indigenous response to European invasion? The most obvious area in which the native resistance was deficient was technology. One reason was that by the second half of the nineteenth century, the technological revolution in armaments worked against non-Europeans in at least two ways. Unlike the intermediate technology of muskets which meant that in the eighteenth and early nineteenth centuries indigenous forces might actually have arms superiority, later developments meant that they lacked the ability to make spare parts and ammunition. This made them increasingly dependent on European suppliers, part of a general modernizing trend that drove them into debt and ironically pushed them into the arms of the very Europeans they were trying to resist. The encroachment of European influence stimulated social and political disintegration, especially in Egypt, Tunis and Morocco, and China. Elsewhere, well-armed minor chiefs with private access to arms merchants challenged central authority. On the battlefield, reliance on outside supply combined with primitive logistical systems usually translated into desperate ammunition shortages.

A second problem was that, in most cases, indigenous forces simply incorporated modern weapons into familiar tactical systems rather than evolving methods that allowed them to be used to advantage. One of the ironies of imperial warfare is that the relative political and military sophistication which made the Zulu, Ashanti or Dahomian empires so formidable in an African context, or assured Hova domination of Madagascar, rendered them all the more vulnerable to European conquest. In most of these societies, armies and warfare were enmeshed in a very precise social or religious structure. For instance, like the Ashantis, the Dahomian army went into battle in an arc formation. There was nothing intrinsically dysfunctional about an arc – after all, it had worked for Hannibal at Cannae, and inspired the Schlieffen Plan used by the Germans against the French in 1914. However, in the African context, the arc had become a social as much as a military concept. Each man's (or, in the case of the Dahomians, woman's) position in the arc was determined by the importance of his or her chief. To change this would have required a social revolution. Furthermore, they were armies designed for slave raiding, or for short campaigns at the end of which the defeated tribe was not annihilated but integrated into the empire. The arc formation was well adapted to creeping up to a village in the dead of night and pouncing at first light. It also counted one remarkable success against Europeans – a Zulu *impi* in the 'cow horns' configuration enveloped and annihilated a surprised and straggling British force at Isandlwana in 1879. But the prospect of fighting a bloody battle, or a series of battles, against a relentless European invader placed intolerable strains on these armies. Even when the indigenous resistance could achieve surprise, like the Ashanti at Amoatu or the Dahomians at Dogba, they were seldom able to profit from it so long as the defending force kept their discipline. Defeat invited disintegration as armies whose feudal levies carried about two weeks' rations ran out of food, distant family members, sometimes with European connivance, advanced rival claims to the throne, well-armed minor chiefs declared independence, and subject peoples revolted. Indeed, a combination of these events, triggered by a European invasion, often did more than European arms to scupper coherent native resistance.

The inability of indigenous societies to stand toe-to-toe with Western invaders on the battlefield was ultimately a cultural and political problem. With the exception of Meiji Japan, even the most advanced civilizations lacked the ability to adapt to the challenge of Western military encroachment. From the 1860s, Chinese reformers argued that their country should follow the path of self-strengthening and emulate Western technology if China were to maintain its independence both from barbarian domination and internal disorder. The best of them realized, however, that the problem was not merely one of acquiring better technology, but of creating a national structure which could make it effective. China needed an educational system which could produce engineers to run arsenals and shipyards. This required a national strategy administered by a modern civil service whose members were rewarded for something other than a mastery of poetry and calligraphy. Finally, China needed a class of soldier superior to the crude, ignorant and careless bannermen. An arsenal and a shipyard were established in the 1860s that began to turn out guns and ships, as well as trained apprentices, in the next decade. Schools were created which added Western languages and mathematics to the traditional Chinese curriculum of history, literature and composition, and students were sent abroad to Europe, America and Japan for study. These reforms began a process that promised success in modernizing China over the long term. In the short term, however, technical and educational reforms were microscopic experiments dwarfed by the immensity of Chinese backwardness. The fact that they were often inefficiently applied opened them to attack by a tradition-bound civil service and a military at once awed by the power of Western arms, while rejecting them as barbarian imports. Chinese advocates of innovation were themselves denounced as traitorous purveyors of economic and cultural imperialism. The administrators and technicians which these reforms sought to produce challenged a Confucian vision

Hiram Maxim (extreme right) demonstrates the tree-harvesting capabilities of his machine gun to potential Chinese purchasers. As with artillery, however, the Chinese failed to integrate the machine gun into an effective military system.

of a harmonious social order based on hierarchy and standing. Traditionalists argued that it was impossible to be trained in Western ways and retain the moral character required for government service. Finally, a self-strengthening programme, which in the 1860s focused on Chinese defence capabilities, became diverted into wider concerns of industrial and transportation development. In the end, most of the successful reform experiments like the Hunan and Anwhei armies, or the Penang navy, were the product of local initiatives taken not only in the absence of imperial help and encouragement, but often in an atmosphere of official indifference or even hostility. These actually contributed to the demise of the Ch'ing dynasty and the rise of warlordism in twentieth-century China.

Elsewhere, the very primitiveness of some societies, while it may have made them tenacious military opponents, ultimately doomed their resistance. Few of these societies were uniformly hostile to the invader, nor had they the sense of fighting a war of survival. Divided by geography, by rivalries of caste, tribe, clan or family, their bonds of common culture weak, a unified response based on a shared sense of self-interest, when it could be mustered, seldom survived the first military débâcle. For instance, the democratic nature of Amerindian societies made it very difficult to cobble together a common resistance, each group or clan deciding whether it was in its interests to fight or make peace. Aggressive opponents of the Amerindians, like Generals Crook and Miles, exploited these divisions by incorporating Amerindians into their forces. The major advantages were psychological and political rather than operational. 'Nothing breaks them up like turning their own people against them,' wrote Crook of his successful pursuit of Geronimo. 'It is not merely a question of catching them better with Indians, but of a broader and more enduring aim – their disintegration.' Crook and Miles were especially adept in using Indians as agents to stimulate dissent among those eager to continue to fight. Already, the Amerindian response to Western invasion was individual rather than collective. The battlefield was a place where the individual warrior sought glory and plunder. No medals were awarded for discipline and teamwork. The American historian John M. Gates has noted that 'Amerindians were capable only of sporadic violence, guerrillas who, though they displayed flashes of tactical brilliance, were bereft of strategic insight.' This was just as well, as any rational assessment on their part would have revealed the hopelessness of the Amerindian plight. The great historian of the Amerindian wars of the American West, Robert Utley, argues that it was the relentless pressure of European migration, rather than the US Army, which deprived the Amerindian of the land and the sustenance that left him no alternative but to submit.

The most formidable empires were often little more than fragile coalitions of reformers and traditionalists, jihadists and the moderately

Apache chief Geronimo (on horse at left) would leave his family in safety on the reservation while he plundered the countryside, escaping into Mexico when closely pursued.

AMERINDIAN WARS 1860–90

Clashes between White settlers and Amerindians offered a persistent feature of the opening of the American West. However, like other indigenous groups faced with occupation, Amerindian hostility was seldom uniform, but piecemeal and fragmented, some groups co-operating with the invaders, others choosing to resist.

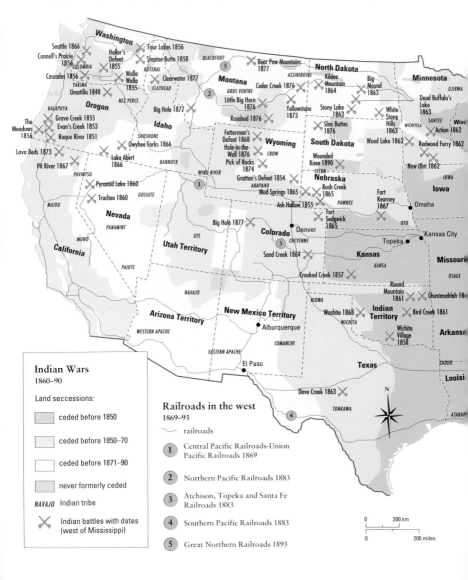

Seattle 1866
Connell's Prairie 1856
Cascades 1856
Umatilla 1848
KALAPUYA
Grave Creek 1855
Evan's Creek 1853
Roque River 1851
The Meadows 1856
Lava Beds 1873
Pit River 1867
PAVIOTSO
Pyramid Lake 1860
Truckee 1860
MAIDU
MONO
California
PANAMINT
PAIUTE
Nevada

Washington
Haller's Defeat 1855
Four Lakes 1856
Steptoe Butte 1858
COLUMBIA
Walla Walla 1855
YAKIMA
Clearwater 1877
FLATHEAD
KUTENAI
NEZ PERCE
Oregon
Big Hole 1877
Idaho
SHOSHONE
Owyhee Forks 1866
Lake Abert 1866
BANNOCK
GOSIUTE
Utah Territory
UTE
NAVAJO

BLACKFOOT
Montana
GROS VENTRE
Little Big Horn 1876
Rosebud 1876
Fetterman's Defeat 1868
Hole-in-the-Wall 1876
Pick of Rocks 1874
WIND RIVER
ARAPAHO
Grattan's Defeat 1854
Mud Springs 1865
Ash Hollow 1855
Big Hole 1877
Colorado
Denver
CHEYENNE
Sand Creek 1864
Crooked Creek 1857
KIOWA
Arizona Territory
WESTERN APACHE
New Mexico Territory
Alburquerque
EASTERN APACHE
El Paso
COMANCHE

Bear Paw Mountains 1877
Cedar Creek 1876
Yellowstone 1873
CROW
Wyoming
TETON
South Dakota
Wounded Knee 1890
Nebraska
Rush Creek 1865
PAWNEE
Fort Sedgwick 1865
Fort Kearney 1867

ASSINIBOINE
Kildee Mountain 1864
Stony Lake 1863
Slim Buttes 1876
Wood Lake 1862
North Dakota
Big Mound 1863
White Stone Hills 1863
WICHIYELA
Dead Buffalo's Lake 1863
SANTEE
Action 1862
Redwood Ferry 1862
New Ulm 1862
Minnesota
OJIBWA
WISC
IOWA
Iowa
Omaha
Kansas City
Topeka
Kansas
KANSA
Round Mountain 1861
Chustenahlah 18
OTO
OSAGE
Washita 1868
WICHITA
Wichita Village 1858
Indian Territory
Bird Creek 1861
Arkansa
CADDO
Texas
Dove Creek 1863
TONKAWA
ATAKA
Louisi
Missouri

Indian Wars
1860–90

Land seccessions:

- ceded before 1850
- ceded before 1850–70
- ceded before 1871–90
- never formerly ceded

NAVAJO Indian tribe

✗ Indian battles with dates (west of Mississippi)

Railroads in the west
1869–93

〜 railroads

(1) Central Pacific Railroads-Union Pacific Railroads 1869

(2) Northern Pacific Railroads 1883

(3) Atchison, Topeka and Santa Fe Railroads 1883

(4) Southern Pacific Railroads 1883

(5) Great Northern Railroads 1893

0   200 km

0   200 miles

pious, rulers and subject peoples, or rival family members and competing economic interests. For these reasons, a clever commander with a fine sense of politics like Wellesley in India, Jardine in China, Faidherbe in western Sudan, Gallieni in Tonkin and Madagascar, or Lyautey in Morocco, was able to exploit these differences. Native élites could be co-opted into the imperial system, a royal brother bribed, a subject tribe offered an alliance, all of which injected the virus of disintegration and lowered the morale of those keen to fight by expanding the power of those with the foresight to submit to the new imperial unity. Even in societies with fairly advanced political élites like the Philippines, the contradictions and divisions of the independence movement were significant. As with successful counter-insurgent commanders elsewhere, Frederick Funston's success in Luzon relied on a combination of a hard-hitting military force that harassed and demoralized the guerrillas, with political initiatives that divided his opposition and isolated the diehard revolutionaries. Filipino nationalism, confined largely to a European-educated Luzon élite, was too abstract a concept to serve as a unifying ideology across an archipelago of islands. Nor were the revolutionaries united behind well-defined goals. The upper-class leaders wanted democratic reform. To succeed, however, they needed to mobilize the peasants whose goals were to maintain a traditional society. Many also feared that prolonged revolution might end in military dictatorship. Funston enlisted Ilocano against Tagalog, divided the *ilustrado* leadership by offering reformers among them positions in local government, and appealed to peasant expectations that American rule would lighten the burden of rapacious landlords by building schools and initiating other public works projects.

Few resistance leaders were 'bitter-enders', and many sought accommodation with the European invader, rather than a war to the death. Abd el-Kader was content to replicate a version of Algeria's relationship with the Ottoman Empire, permitting the French to control the Algerian coast so long as they left him alone to organize the tribes of the hinterland. Likewise, by the time Europeans began to

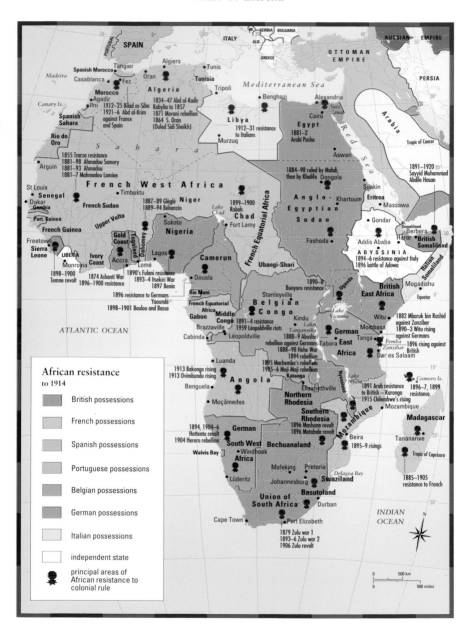

African resistance
to 1914

- British possessions
- French possessions
- Spanish possessions
- Portuguese possessions
- Belgian possessions
- German possessions
- Italian possessions
- independent state
- principal areas of African resistance to colonial rule

SPAIN

PORTUGAL

ITALY

SERBIA   BULGARIA

GREECE

ALB.

RUSSIAN   EMPIRE

Madeira

Tangier

Algiers

Tunis

Mediterranean Sea

PERSIA

Spanish Morocco

Casablanca

Oran

Tunisia

Tripoli

Benghazi

Alexandria

Suez Canal

Arabia

Fez

Morocco

Agadir

Ifni

Algeria

1834–47 Abd al-Kadir
Kabylia to 1857
1871 Morani rebellion
1864 S. Oran
(Ouled Sidi Sheikh)

Cairo

Egypt
1881–2
Arabi Pasha

Red Sea

Tropic of Cancer

Canary Is.

1912–25 Bilad as-Siba against France
1921–6 Abd al-Krim against France and Spain

Spanish
Sahara

Libya
1912–31 resistance
to Italians

Murzuq

Aswan

1891–1920
Sayyid Muhammad
Abdile Hasan

Rio do
Oro

Arguin

S a h a r a

1855 Trarza resistance
1881–98 Ahmadou Samory
1881–93 Ahmadou
1881–7 Mahmadou Lamine

1884–98 ruled by Mahdi, then by Khalifa   Dongola

Suakin

Eritrea

St Louis

Dakar

Senegal

Gambia

Port. Guinea

French Guinea

F r e n c h   W e s t   A f r i c a

Timbuktu

Niger

French Sudan

1887–89 Glégé
1889–94 Behanzin

Sokoto

Lake
Chad

1899–1900
Rabah

Chad

Fort Lamy

A n g l o -
E g y p t i a n
S u d a n

Khartoum

Fashoda

Massawa

Gondar

Somaliland
Berbera
Harar

British
Somaliland

Upper Volta

Gold
Coast

Nigeria

A B Y S S I N I A
1894–6 resistance against Italy
1896 battle of Adowa

Italian
Somaliland

Freetown
Sierra
Leone

LIBERIA

Monrovia

Ivory
Coast

Accra

Lagos

Camerun

Addis Ababa

Mogadishu

Equator

1898–1900
Temne revolt

1874 Ashanti War
1896–1900 resistance

Togoland

Dahomey

Lomé

1890's Fulani resistance
1893–4 Itsekiri War
1897 Benin

Douala

Ubangi-Shari

1890–8
Bunyoro resistance

British
East Africa

Uganda

1896 resistance to Germans

Yaoundé

1898–1901 Boulou and Bassa

Rio Muni

French Equatorial
Africa

Gabon

Middle
Congo

Brazzaville

Cabinda

Stanleyville

B e l g i a n
C o n g o

Kindu

1891–4 resistance
1959 Léopoldville riots

Léopoldville

Lake
Victoria

Lake
Tanganyika

Witu

German
East
Africa

Mombasa

Tanga

Pemba

Zanzibar

1882 Mbaruk bin Rashid
against Zanzibar
1890–3 Witu rising
against Germans

1896 rising against
British

ATLANTIC OCEAN

1888–9 Abushiri
rebellion against Germans
1888–98 Hehe War
1894 rebellion
1895 Machemba's rebellion
1905–6 Maji-Maji rebellion

Tabora

Dar es Salaam

Comoro Is.

Luanda

Katanga

Lake
Nyasa

1891 Arab resistance
to British – Karonga
1915 Chilembwe's rising

1896–7, 1899
resistance

1913 Bakongo rising
1913 Ovimbundu rising

A n g o l a

Elisabethville

Mozambique

Benguela

Moçâmedes

Northern
Rhodesia

Southern
Rhodesia

Mozambique

Beira

1895–9 risings

Madagascar

Tananarive

1894, 1904–6
Hottento revolt
1904 Herero rebellion

German

South West

Africa

Walvis Bay

1896 Mashona revolt
1896 Matabele revolt

Bechuanaland

Tropic of Capricorn

Windhoek

Mafeking

Pretoria

Johannesburg

Swaziland

Delagoa Bay

1885–1905
resistance to French

Lüderitz

Union of
South Africa

Basutoland

Durban

INDIAN
OCEAN

Cape Town

Port Elizabeth

1879 Zulu war 1
1893–6 Zulu war 2
1906 Zulu revolt

0   500 km

0   500 miles

N

AFRICAN RESISTANCE TO 1914

In the last quarter of the nineteenth century, European imperialism achieved an unstoppable momentum as Africa was sliced into national segments by ambitious soldiers and colonial administrators. Indigenous resistance, though often courageous, was seldom effective. In fact, more Africans fought for European imperialists than against them. By the turn of the century, only Abyssinia and Morocco retained a tenuous independence.

invade sub-Saharan Africa, the old *jihad* empires of western Sudan had passed their peak and had begun to break up. And even at their height, these religiously inspired states had been forced to make compromises to accommodate a diverse group of peoples, customs and leaders. Ashanti leaders signed a treaty with the British after Amoafo. Dahomian leaders attempted to negotiate peace with the French General Dodds who refused because he believed that 'King Behanzin only looks to trick us and gain time'.

Examples of successful resistance in the late nineteenth century are few and very much tied to the contingency of local circumstance. Afghanistan offers an exception to the norm of unsuccessful resistance to European encroachment. The British twice invaded Afghanistan in the nineteenth century because they feared that Russian machinations there would destabilize India. In 1839, New Delhi aimed to install a friendly regime in Kabul, in the process solidifying British influence in the Sind and the Sikh-dominated Punjab. An invasion force grabbed Kabul with little opposition, and placed Shah Shuja on the throne. However, the new king's British provenance combined with the perceived moral laxity of his regime to undermine his credibility with mullahs and fiercely independent Afghan tribesmen. An inept military occupation by Waterloo veteran Major-General William Elphinstone failed to cope with the growing disorder. In January 1842, 4,500 soldiers of the Kabul garrison were massacred as they tried to regain the Kyber Pass. A British force returned to Kabul in September of that year to liberate prisoners, chastise rebel *sidars* (tribal chiefs), and, in the words of Wellington, teach Muslims 'from Peking to Constantinople' that British power could not be trifled with. Having thus restored British military honor, they marched back to India the following month. But the failure of British policy in Afghanistan sparked wars with the Sind and the Sikhs that took until 1849 to quell.

Barely twenty-six years later, Russian advances in Central Asia combined with renewed instability in Afghanistan to invite a return of British forces in late 1878. This time London's goal was to depose the king Amir Sher Ali, 'a savage with a touch of insanity', according to the Viceroy Edward Bulwer Lytton, destroy his army, and break up the country into manageable kingdoms. British commanders were confident that, unlike the First Afghan War, the repeating rifle and modern artillery would give the invaders an unbeatable technological edge over the Afghans armed with antique *jezails*. As in 1839, the British invasion force had little trouble

Afghans armed with long-barrelled jezails, *whose range easily outdistanced European muskets in the early nineteenth century. European armies found that the close-order formations and volley-firing techniques that worked well in a European setting were impotent against indigenous peoples firing from concealed positions.*

installing itself in Afghanistan's major cities. Unfortunately for the British, Sher Ali's flight and subsequent death left the victors with no one with whom to negotiate. As often in imperial campaigns, opposition was slow to mobilize. But by late 1880, Afghan tribesmen had defeated a British force at Maiwand, had the British locked into the major towns, and were busy murdering anyone foolish enough to cooperate with them. The deteriorating situation in Afghanistan combined with the victory of Gladstone's anti-imperialist Liberals in the 1880 elections left Lytton desperate for an exit strategy. He negotiated a quick deal with Amir Abdur Rahman on the back of thumping victories over Afghan forces by General Roberts at Kabul and Kandahar, gave him arms and money to sustain his regime, and vacated the country in May 1881.

The British failed to achieve their goals in either of these wars not so much because Afghan resistance was overwhelming, but because it proved so tenacious. Well-led British forces seldom had a problem defeating Afghans in open combat, any more than would the Russians in the 1980s. But the problem of Afghanistan from an imperial perspective was that no quick fix existed to speed the transition from resistance to compliance. Islam allied with the appearance of the *feringhi* (foreigner) to import a glimmer of fleeting unity into what was little more than a primitive aggregation of congenitally anarchical, religiously intolerant hill clans for whom feuding, combat and treachery was a job description. No Afghan government with the slightest taint of collaboration could anticipate a fate other than assassination and eventual overthrow. The problem for the military commander was that Afghanistan offered no prize worth taking, no center of gravity whose seizure would end opposition. To possess the major towns, capture or kill a major leader, or cut wide swathes through his followers, only energized resistance. No doubt the British, like the French in Algeria or the Russians in Chechnya, could have conquered the country had they been prepared to commit large numbers of forces to a devastating campaign lasting years, if not decades. However, the Russian advance in Central Asia in the 1860s removed the economic incentive for conquest that had fueled in part the

British invasion of 1839, while Anglo-Russian détentes in 1844, 1878 and 1907 temporarily took Afghanistan off the table as an issue of strategic competition. Otherwise, the vast and tortured geography of the country, the implacable mentality of the population, combined with the inevitable opposition a prolonged campaign of conquest would have evoked in the British public, to make Afghanistan a high-risk investment simply not worth contemplating.

Probably the most remarkable resistance leader in the late nineteenth century, one to rank with Abd el-Kader and Shamil, was a merchant from the upper Niger basin named Samori Touré. In 1851 Samori deserted his trade and for the next twenty years lived as a war chief in the service of several African leaders. In the 1870s, he struck out on his own, to create an empire that stretched from the right bank of the Niger, south to Sierra Leone and Liberia. Islam gave Samori's empire a veneer of ideological unity. But the real solidity of Samori's dominion resided in his formidable military organization. His territories were divided into ten provinces, eight of which raised an army corps of 4–5,000 professional *sofas* or warriors, supplemented by conscription. In peacetime, all *sofas* trained for half the year and engaged in agricultural work the other six months. Samori kept two élite contingents of 500 men in each of the two provinces that he ruled directly, from which he drew his officers for his provincial corps. The corps, which contained both cavalry and infantry, were organized down to squad level. On campaign, three army corps usually advanced in an

A sofa or warrior in the army of Samori Touré. Samori arguably organized the most successful African resistance to European encroachment. His army was solidly organized, well armed, and tactically sophisticated. A scorched-earth defence strategy complemented a skilful diplomacy that kept his empire intact and his French enemy at bay for seventeen years.

arc formation, fairly typical for West Africa, while a fourth corps was held in reserve. This military empire was sustained by taxes, usually paid in agricultural produce. Hard currency to purchase arms in Sierra Leone was earned by slave trading and from the gold fields of Bure.

Samori managed to unify an empire that survived for almost two decades against repeated French advances. Early in the 1880s, he understood that French discipline and firepower made set-piece engagements suicidal. Therefore, he adopted guerrilla warfare, shifting his frontiers to allow him to collect the harvest, while forcing the French to advance across land depopulated and thoroughly burned over by his *sofas*. His troops, masters of the ambush and equipped with an estimated 8,000 repeating rifles, then struck at the over-extended French columns. After a particularly bloody skirmish with Samori's *sofas* in the Diamanko marshes in January 1892, Colonel Gustave Humbert conceded that Samori's troops 'fight exactly like Europeans, with less discipline perhaps, but with much greater determination'. Samori's scorched-earth tactic evened the odds against him, because it forced the French to reduce their columns to around 1,000 men, which was about all French logistics could support. Logistical difficulties contributed to the French defeat, with heavy casualties at the hands of Samori before Kong in 1895. But remarkable as his political and military skills were, Samori's accomplishments must not be exaggerated. His longevity – he was surprised in his camp and captured by a French column only in 1898 – owed more to French disorganization than to his own skill.

French advances came in fits and starts. There were several reasons for this. There was a constant turnover of French commanders, all of whom underestimated their opponent. The French advance in West Africa was characterized by constant friction between Paris, which was not keen to advance the boundaries of empire, and local commanders who were. Financial constraints delayed French advances against Samori, as did the requirement that the French, never numerous, also fight other opponents in the Niger region, in particular the Tokolor empire. Samori also gained some residual support from the British in

The Ethiopian victory at Adowa in 1896 owed something to the adaptation to modern arms after 1885, when the traditional phalanx gave way to loose formations which approached by fire and encirclement. The great irony, however, was that, had the Italians delayed their attack for a few days, the Ethiopian force would have consumed their rations and been forced to disperse.

Sierra Leone and the Gambia. Nor was Samori a 'bitter-ender'. He recognized that eventually he must accept a French protectorate. It was France's unwillingness to negotiate, rather than Samori's commitment to total war, that also protracted the struggle.

Ethiopian resistance owed much to a semi-successful adaptation of technology, to the incompetence of the enemy, and to luck. The influx of modern arms caused the Ethiopians to abandon their traditional phalanx attack in 1885 in favour of loose formations that approached by fire and encirclement. Nevertheless, their successful resistance at Adowa owed less to the mastery of modern tactics by Menelik's largely feudal levies than to the extraordinary incompetence of General Baratieri, who allowed himself to be goaded into a premature attack by his subordinate officers and by the stinging rebukes of Italian Prime Minister Francesco Crispi, who had dispatched his successor from Italy. Rather than wait a few days until the Ethiopian soldiers inevitably consumed their meagre rations and would have been forced to disperse, he ordered his 15,000 troops forward in three separate columns, only for them to be overwhelmed piecemeal by 100,000 Ethiopians.

After a series of unsuccessful rebellions in the last quarter of the nineteenth century, Cuban revolutionaries succeeded in shaking off Spanish rule for several reasons. A severe economic recession, beginning in 1895, had created a climate of discontent. When, in July 1895, Cuban revolutionaries proclaimed a moratorium on all economic activity, aimed principally at the planter and commercial classes, the traditional pillars of Spanish colonialism, the government response was at once brutal and ineffective. Madrid dispatched General Valeriano Weyler with reinforcements to swell the Spanish garrison in Cuba to 200,000 troops. Weyler immediately ordered Cuba's rural population to be reconcentrated in the towns, and forbade commerce between the towns and the countryside. The Spanish army scoured the countryside destroying food stocks, slaughtering livestock that could not be herded towards the towns, and burning villages from which the insurgents might gain support. Rather than face the prospect of a dismal and possibly fatal existence in towns where nothing had been prepared to receive them, many previously neutral peasants fled to the hills to join the insurgents, whose numbers rose to about 50,000. In the meantime, by concentrating his forces in defensive positions in the urban areas, Weyler left the plantations undefended and vulnerable to *la tea* – the torch – which was the insurgents' principal means of intimidation. The result was a military stalemate in a war where the enemies seldom traded shots: 'the Spanish assaulted the peasants, the Cubans assailed the planters', one historian writes. 'Both attacked property.'

In the long run, Weyler's strategy was doomed to failure because it did not have an offensive component, either military or political. His army lacked the size and striking power to restore control over at least some portions of the countryside, reanimate economic activity, and isolate and damage rebel forces. Politically, he alienated a vast middle ground of moderate Autonomist opinion which traditionally had condemned the abuses of Spanish rule rather than argued for independence *per se*. Weyler herded them into prison, drove them into exile or into the arms of the independence factions. By 1897, faith in victory had been shaken even among loyalists who faced financial ruin. No peasants remained to harvest the sugar crop, and no troops were assigned to protect those plantations which did attempt to gather crops from *la tea*. Planters who could afford it recruited guards to protect their property. Those who could not – which was most of them – left their crops to rot in the fields, or be harvested by the insurgents. Weyler also managed to alienate the powerful Havana tobacco industry in May 1896 when, in an attempt to punish cigar centres in Florida which were hotbeds of separatist opinion, he prohibited the export of leaf tobacco to the United States. Inflation soared as food became scarce and the government recklessly printed paper money.

Weyler began to abandon the smaller provincial cities, sometimes in the face of insurgent assault, and consolidated his forces in the larger towns where 'reconcentrated' peasants were dying by scores. Having pushed the Autonomists into the arms of the separatists, Weyler tossed loyalists into the arms of the United States, which they began to see as their only salvation from certain dispossession by a victorious, socially radical insurgent army. Therefore, in the eyes of Cuban nationalist historians at least, US intervention, ostensibly against Spain, was in reality directed against the insurgency, and snatched a victory which would have fallen to it in the fullness of time. In reality, however, the motives for American intervention were far more complex and idealistic. Washington would have been quite content for Spain to continue to administer Cuba, but had become frustrated over Madrid's inability to resolve peacefully the crises that had racked the island for almost thirty years. The explosion of the USS *Maine* in Havana harbour, although certainly no fault of the Spanish, brought together very diverse interests to argue for intervention, led by humanitarians outraged by Weyler's concentration camps. They were joined by those eager to promote democracy in Latin America, businessmen with

Theodore Roosevelt's 'Rough Riders' fill their cartridge belts as they prepare for action in Cuba, 1898. The Spanish-American War set the United States on the road to a seaborne empire of which Roosevelt was one of the greatest protagonists.

property in Cuba, and navalists upset by Spanish searches of US ships on the high seas and keen to clear European outposts from the Caribbean in preparation for the building of the Panama Canal.

Boer resistance appears to have been of a tenacity that defies the rule of unsuccessful resistance to imperial power. On closer examination, however, it adhered more closely to the common pattern – Amerindian, Algerian or African – of the fanatical few determined to fight on after the main Boer army had been defeated and the majority of the Boer people reduced to a state of neutrality. Indeed, the Boer strategy for avoiding national collapse after Bloemfontein was to shed those whose commitment was lukewarm and to fight on with only a hard core in the hope that the British would eventually give up. So skilful was Jakob Morenga in eluding German forces in South-West Africa between 1904 and 1906 that he earned the nickname of the 'Black de Wet'. But German pursuit ultimately forced him to seek refuge in the Cape Colony where he was interned, and eventually killed, by the British.

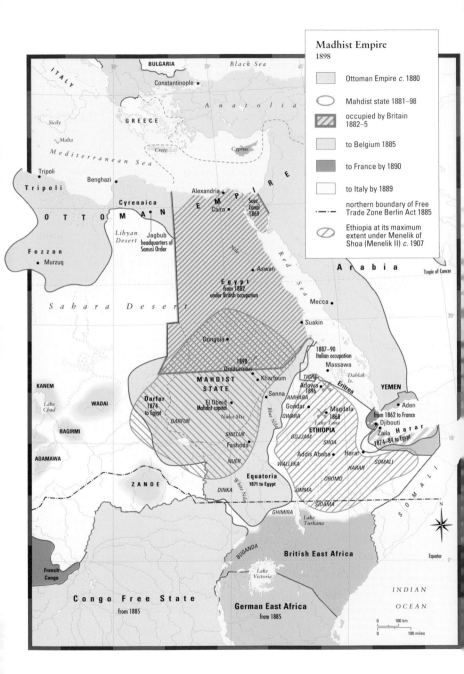

Madhist Empire
1898

Ottoman Empire *c.* 1880

Mahdist state 1881–98

occupied by Britain 1882–5

to Belgium 1885

to France by 1890

to Italy by 1889

northern boundary of Free Trade Zone Berlin Act 1885

Ethiopia at its maximum extent under Menelik of Shoa (Menelik II) *c.* 1907

ITALY

BULGARIA

Black Sea

Constantinople •

Anatolia

GREECE

Sicily

• Malta

Crete

Cyprus

Mediterranean Sea

Tripoli •

• Benghazi

Alexandria •

Cairo •

Suez Canal 1869

EMPIRE

Arabia

Tropic of Cancer

Tripoli

Cyrenaica

O T T O M A N

Libyan Desert

Jagbub headquarters of Sanusi Order

• Aswan

Red Sea

Fezzan

• Murzuq

Sahara   Desert

Egypt
from 1882
under British occupation

• Mecca

20°

• Suakin

• Dongola

1887–90
Italian occupation

Massawa

KANEM

Lake Chad

WADAI

BAGIRMI

ADAMAWA

1898

Omdurman •

MAHDIST STATE

• Khartoum

TIGRE

Adowa 1896

Senna •

AMHARA

Eritrea

Dahlak Is.

YEMEN

• Aden

Darfur
1874
to Egypt

El Obeid •
Mahdist capital

Gondar •

QWARA

Magdala
1868
Lake Tana

from 1862 to France

Djibouti

DARFUR

Nuba Mts

Blue Nile

BOJJAM

ETHIOPIA

SHOA

Zaila

Harar

1874–84 to Egypt

SHILLUK

Fashoda •

WALLEKA

Addis Ababa •

• Harar

HARAR

SOMALI

NUER

Equatoria
1871 to Egypt

White Nile

DINKA

JIMMA

OROMO

S O M A L I

ZANDE

GHIMIRA

SIDAMA

Lake Turkana

N

BUGANDA

British East Africa

Lake Victoria

Equator

French Congo

C o n g o   F r e e   S t a t e
from 1885

German East Africa
from 1885

INDIAN

OCEAN

0   100 km

0   100 miles

Western invaders had been successful during this phase of imperial warfare basically because, unlike the American or South American revolutions, or the Mexican resistance to the French, indigenous societies lacked the power or the cohesion to resist their persistent encroachment. Also, for most of the nineteenth century, rival imperial powers refrained from coming to the aid of the indigenous fighters, beyond selling them a few surplus rifles. So small wars remained small. The most persistent rivalry was between Britain and France, and in 1898 it nearly erupted into war. Paris had been particularly irked when the British had occupied Egypt in 1882 and declared it a protectorate. The southern frontier of Egypt was somewhat in dispute, however, after the British abandoned the upper Nile to the Sudanese Mahdi and his successors in 1885. Therefore, the upper Nile was effectively unoccupied by a European power. In 1896, French colonialists dispatched Colonel Jean-Baptiste Marchand with a handful of French marine officers and around 200 hand-picked Senegalese riflemen up the mouth of the Congo river. Two years and 3,000 miles later, Marchand reached the Nile at a placed called Fashoda, a small collection of mud buildings several hundred miles upriver from Khartoum. With as much ceremony as they could muster, the French broke out the white dress uniforms which they had brought for this occasion, and planted their tricolour flag. France had reasserted her historic claims on the Nile.

The bellicose colonialist in charge of the British Colonial Office, Joseph Chamberlain, was in no mood to tolerate a French attempt to work its way back into Egypt and threaten British control of the Suez

THE MAHDIST EMPIRE 1898

London had greeted news of the rise of the Mahdist empire in the early 1880s with mild indifference. Charles 'Chinese' Gordon's death in Khartoum in 1885 had embarrassed Gladstone, who had ordered Gordon to evacuate the garrison, not perish with it. But, generally speaking, the death of a soldier at the hands of savages, while regrettable, was treated as an occupational hazard. The arrival of the Marchand expedition at Fashoda in 1898 abruptly changed the equation. News of a French rival at Fashoda precipitated the British advance to pre-empt a French claim on the upper Nile.

Canal. Already, a British–Egyptian expedition had begun to encroach on the Mahdi's empire. On 1 September 1898, General Horatio Kitchener arrived at Omdurman, across the Nile from Khartoum, with a force of over 20,000 men, gunboats mounting 100 guns, and a vast supply convoy of camels and horses. On the following morning at dawn, in the shadow of the great dome of the Mahdi's tomb, 50,000 Sudanese tribesmen in a line four miles long attacked the British. They were massacred. As Kitchener surveyed the 10,000 bodies that lay in piles over the desert, he was handed an envelope with urgent orders from England to proceed up the Nile in all haste to dislodge a French force at Fashoda. Kitchener gathered two battalions of Sudanese, one hundred Cameron Highlanders, a battery of artillery and four Maxim guns in five riverboats which steamed under an Egyptian flag. As Kitchener approached Fashoda on 18 September, he sent a messenger with an invitation for Marchand to dine aboard his flagship. With great courtesy, Kitchener, wearing an Egyptian fez, complimented the French colonel on his splendid march, but added that he must protest the French presence on the Nile. The Frenchman

'The Flight of the Khalifa after his Defeat at the Battle of Omdurman, 2 September 1898' by Robert Kelly.

replied that he intended to defend himself if attacked. The two men agreed to allow their respective governments to sort out matters.

The Fashoda crisis was eventually resolved, but not without acrimony. The press of the two countries swapped vituperative insults. The French moved reinforcements to their Mediterranean coast and made plans to defend Corsica, which they calculated the British would attack if war came. Eventually the French gave way. Marchand was in an impossible situation. He struck his colours on 11 December 1898. However, he declined the British offer to exit via a Nile steamer and instead marched to the Red Sea where his expedition was collected by a French warship. The Fashoda crisis did have a silver lining for French colonialists, however. Quiet negotiations between London and Paris eventually culminated in the signing of the Entente Cordiale of 1904, which bartered British recognition of a French free hand in Morocco against Parisian acquiescence to London's domination of Egypt. Yet the fact that the two greatest colonial powers had nearly gone to war over a flyblown sand-bank on the upper Nile was, for many, a wake-up call. 'We have behaved like madmen in Africa,' French President Félix Faure complained in the wake of the Fashoda crisis, 'led astray by irresponsible people called the colonialists.'

In retrospect, however, Fashoda was the end of an era. Clashes between competing imperial powers had been muted because it was in the interests of no-one to destabilize the international equilibrium merely to lay claim to a few thousand acres of scrub, jungle or desert. Because European expansion abroad appeared to have only a minimal effect on the European balance of power, governments were able to contain the ambitions of their more exuberant imperialists when they exceeded the bounds of prudence. Besides, when conflict arose, there was always enough land to trade to allow every power to escape with its dignity intact. But if Faure believed that the madness of colonialism was a thing of the past, he was mistaken. As the twentieth century dawned, imperial warfare would become more, not less, destructive as rivalries between the great powers would up the stakes in the game of imperial conquest.

CHAPTER FOUR

Upping the Stakes: the Limits of Imperial Warfare

Boer Burghers formed a people's army, organized into commandos of 500 to 2,000 men behind elected leaders. They operated as mounted infantry, fighting on foot, fleeing on their ponies when pressed. Armed with 37,000 Mauser rifles purchased by the Transvaal government with the revenues of the gold fields, the Boers proved remarkable marksmen.

Upping the Stakes:
the Limits of Imperial Warfare

Politically, for almost thirty years, imperial expansion had been achieved on the cheap. For a minimum investment of cash and manpower, some European nations had extended their control over vast stretches of the world. On the whole, it had been a low-risk venture which European publics could follow like a sporting event. European governments could indulge at little expense the soldier's appetite for glory, the missionary's yearning for souls to convert, the reformer's passion for improvement, and the nationalist's clamour for trophy lands to invigorate national self-esteem. There was land enough to satisfy every active imperial power, so that competition was kept to a minimum. As a Continental power, France was acutely conscious of the dangers of imperial overstretch. Hence, although French and British interests did clash in Africa in the 1890s, Paris was obliged to resolve each crisis in favour of her European commitments. Until 1905 Germany seemed content with a fairly small slice of the imperial pie. The United States focused on consolidating its western frontier until 1898, and barring outsiders from Latin America. Russia had its own near-abroad in Central Asia to secure. Until the Sino-Japanese War of 1894–5, Japan raced to repair the dilapidation of centuries of self-imposed isolation. While the wars fought to obtain colonial possessions had often been dramatic, occasionally bloody, few imperial nations had invested more than a fraction of their military assets in small wars. A spot of sea power and the occasional punitive expedition was sufficient to influence the behaviour even of elephantine China. Occasional military setbacks did occur. But these were hardly more than transient embarrassments which helped to keep small wars in the forefront of the public mind by making them seem like dangerous adventures. Because these defeats were inflicted at the hands of indigenous, rather than European, opponents, national pride was less likely to be whipped into a frenzy.

As the nineteenth century neared its finale, however, what had been regarded as a more or less casual partition of the world between Britain, France and Russia became far more destabilizing, for two reasons. First, in South Africa Britain confronted an opponent whose tenacity required a military exertion on a scale not witnessed since the Napoleonic wars. Because the Second Boer War of 1899–1902 was fought in the context of the evolving security situation in Europe and the Far East, London for the first time had to deal with the problem of imperial overstretch in an increasingly complex international environment. The reason for this was tied to the second factor that made imperial expansion fraught with risks. The traditional imperial

A Boer commando rides through Johannesburg in a show of political intimidation during the political crisis provoked by the Jameson Raid of 1896. Cecil Rhodes orchestrated the raid in an unsuccessful attempt to spark a rebellion against the Transvaal government by the substantial number of British working in the gold mines.

powers of Russia, Britain and France were challenged by the advent of two new and very aggressive powers eager to break into their quasi-imperial monopoly – Japan and Germany. Since the Meiji Restoration of 1868, Tokyo had struggled to recover ground lost by centuries of self-imposed isolation. By the 1890s, Japan's modernization programme had put the country in a position to lay claim to a sphere of influence in the Far East. Germany, liberated from the moderating influence of Bismarck, demanded a place in the sun to include a large navy and more colonies in Africa. This radically altered the politics of imperialism because small wars now risked becoming large ones. During the nineteenth century the imperial enterprise had been regarded as a triumph of Western civilization; in the early years of the twentieth century it seemed that imperial competition might immolate that very civilization in a gigantic conflagration.

The Boer War

Hardly had the British dodged the bullets of war with France over Fashoda in 1898 than it ploughed into a particularly stubborn enemy in southern Africa. The Second South African War would require a substantial mobilization of British land and naval assets, expose the bankruptcy of a foreign policy anchored in the arrogance of 'splendid isolation', and test popular support for imperialism in Britain. More than any other imperial opponent, the Boers stretched the operational and tactical capabilities of the British Army to the limit. Imperial warfare also revealed its tactical limitations. Callwell noted that, 'in small wars, guerrilla warfare is what the regular armies always have most to dread, and when this is directed by a leader with a genius for war, an effective campaign becomes well-nigh impossible'. Such was the hard lesson learned by the British in a war which the historian Thomas Pakenham has called 'the longest, bloodiest, costliest war Britain fought between 1815 and 1914 – and the most humiliating one since George Washington sent the Redcoats packing in 1783'. Over two and a half years Britain required £200 million, 448,435 British and imperial troops and 22,000 dead to master a farmers' rebellion. This was no longer imperial conquest on the cheap, and British public opinion began to question whether the costs exceeded the benefits.

The origins of the Second South African War were the subject of a polemic from the moment it broke out. Anti-imperialists, and subsequently Marxists, saw the war as the product of a capitalist conspiracy to gain control through force of arms of the gold and diamonds of the Orange Free State and the Transvaal. More modern

THE BOER WAR 1895–1902

The Second South African, or Boer, War was the single most challenging imperial conflict fought by Britain since the eighteenth century. After the early setbacks of 'Black Week', the British army recovered to defeat the main Boer armies and occupy the principal towns. However, 17,000 Boer 'bitter-enders' took to the veld to fight a desperate guerrilla war that lasted another two years.

Boer War 1895–1902

- Boer republics
- Jameson raid 1895
- main line of British advance
- major Boer raids 1899–1901
- battle

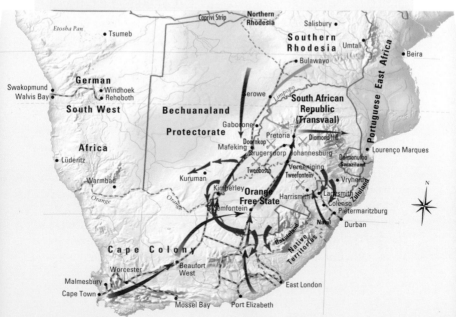

interpretations see British policy as one hijacked by fervent imperialists led by Cecil Rhodes who feared that the newly discovered riches of the Boer republics would derail an imperial scenario which saw the Boer territories eventually absorbed by the British-controlled Cape Colony. Wealth allowed the Boer republics to slip the leash of British tutelage and pursue an independent foreign policy, one that eventually threatened to open the door to German control over the vital Cape route to India.

Although relations between Cape Town and the Boer republics for some time had slithered toward breakdown, the outbreak of war in October 1899 found the British remarkably unprepared. The Conservative government of Lord Salisbury feared that even a whisper of military preparation might transform the tense situation in South Africa into a partisan issue. Rather than prepare in secret for hostilities with the Boers which monthly appeared more likely to break out, Whitehall immersed itself in a bureaucratic war whose main protagonists were the African troops of the commander-in-chief Lord Garnet Wolseley, and the Indian forces of Field Marshal Lord Roberts

of Kandahar. The theatre commander in the Cape, General Sir Redvers Buller, had neither the confidence of Wolseley nor of the War Minister, Lord Lansdowne. Despite the fact that the Boers had inflicted a humiliating defeat on the British at Majuba Hill during the First South African War of 1881, the Boer republics were discounted as serious opponents – British military intelligence thought the Boers capable only of mustering 3,000 men for small-scale raids into the Cape

Field Marshal Lord Roberts of Kandahar assumed command in South Africa in the wake of 'Black Week'. Roberts headed a clique of 'Indian' officers whose war against 'Africans', represented by Redvers Buller, was as intense as that pursued against the Boers.

Colony and Natal, when, in fact, they proved able to throw nearly 30,000 mounted men into Natal alone. Wolseley believed, and Lansdowne agreed, that a garrison of 20,000 would more than suffice to defend British South Africa, half of which was pre-positioned at Ladysmith and Dundee north of the Tugela river in northern Natal. The Foreign Office believed that the Orange Free State could be induced to remain neutral should war occur, thereby isolating the Transvaal. Nearly everyone on the British side, including the deputy prime minister A. J. Balfour, Joseph Chamberlain, the Secretary for the Colonies, and *The Times*, was ruled by complacency. The British entered the war with neither a war plan nor adequate maps of the theatre of operations.

The Boers took the offensive at the outbreak of war, snatching 100 miles of Cape Colony and moving into Natal as far south as the Tugela river. Mafeking and Kimberley became British islands in a Boer-dominated veld, while in Natal, the Dundee garrison was forced back on Ladysmith, and locked in by besieging Boers. By December 1899, Buller had gathered four divisions totalling 60,000 troops and 150 guns to relieve Kimberley and Ladysmith. On 10 December, a British column riding for the strategic railway junction at Stormberg was ambushed by mounted Boers who killed or captured 700 British soldiers. The next day, a frontal attack backed by artillery was scythed down by entrenched Boer marksmen at Magersfontein, about 15 miles south of Kimberley. Finally, on 15 December at Colenso, 4,000 Boers armed with magazine-fed Mauser rifles and well entrenched on the heights on the north bank of the Tugela thwarted an attempt by 16,000 British troops under Buller to break through to Ladysmith. 'Black Week' seemed a totally appropriate name for the five short days during which British forces had suffered almost 7,000 casualties and achieved no strategic results.

Shaken from its complacency, the British government dispatched more troops to South Africa, mobilized the reserves, and called for volunteers, both in Britain and in the white dominions of Canada, Australia and New Zealand. Eventually almost 450,000 men would serve in the British forces in South Africa, against around 87,000 Boers. Lord Roberts was dispatched as commander-in-chief, while Buller's command shrank to the Natal front. In February 1900, Buller succeeded in his fourth attempt to break through to Ladysmith, the same month that Roberts took Kimberley, in the process surrounding the Boer army which had besieged the town. On 13 March, Roberts captured Bloemfontein, capital of the Orange Free State, and offered an amnesty for all except the Boer leaders. Johannesburg fell in late May, and Pretoria barely a week later.

Although ultimately triumphant, the British had demonstrated significant military weaknesses – tactical, logistical and strategic – in this early phase of the war. British forces predictably advanced along railway lines until they met the enemy. Then, they invariably launched unimaginative frontal assaults against Boer positions. Although frontal assaults had worked well enough against disorganized and ill-armed Africans, the price exacted by the Boers, who were both well armed and entrenched, was significant enough to provoke reflection even among the dullest of British generals. Artillery had proven powerless to shake the aim of marksmen dug into rifle pits. Indeed, at Magersfontein the British had suffered numerous casualties from friendly artillery fire. Once the Boer armies besieging Kimberley had been flushed into the open, however, artillery contributed to the surrender of Cronje's force, laagered in a bend in the Modder river and pounded into submission. Logistics and medical services, the key to the success of both Wolseley in Ashanti and Dodds in Dahomey, were neglected, reducing British mobility and raising the casualty rate – 16,168 of 22,000 British dead during the war perished from wounds and disease. The strategic assumptions of the war had been as faulty as the operational and tactical ones. Unfortunately for the British, the defeat of the major Boer armies, the capture of the capitals of the Boer republics and their annexation into the British Empire did not end resistance. The 17,000 or so Boer commandos still at large took to the veld to pursue a guerrilla war which was to last another two years.

A 12-span mule cart belonging to de Wet's commando crosses the Orange river. After the fall of Bloemfontein in March 1900, de Wet, considered the most elusive of Boer guerrillas, abolished wagon trains in the Boer army. Those that remained were gradually gathered in during Kitchener's 'drives'.

In this type of mobile war, the British faced the usual array of disadvantages which had plagued European troops in Africa. Their enemies were unified by a religious belief in the justice of their cause, were extremely self-reliant, hardened to life in the saddle, and were excellent marksmen. In Botha, Delarey, de Wet and Smuts, Boer 'bitter-enders' possessed leaders of great competence. In contrast, British columns were ponderous and lacked adequate co-ordination because of poor staff work, inadequate maps, and faulty communications. Over 2,000 foreigners travelled to South Africa to join the Boer ranks. And while these foreign recruits were of marginal military utility, especially as some quickly became disillusioned by Boer religiosity and racism, their presence indicated a sympathy for the cause of the Boer underdog in Europe. Throughout the war, Boer scouting and intelligence gathering remained superior to that of the British. The imported Australian,

Christiaan de Wet commanded the Orange Free State forces in 1899. He became the most audacious of the Boer commanders and the principal architect of Boer strategy during the guerrilla phase of the war. He gave up trying to block the British advance from the spring of 1900, and instead he concentrated on attacking their lines of communications, especially the railroads.

English and Argentine horses of the British mounted troops could not match in rusticity and endurance those of the Boers, who also took better care of their mounts.

Nevertheless, the Boers had weaknesses: Boer commanders found it difficult to co-ordinate strategy and exploit success, even to issue simple orders, with troops who were so fiercely independent. The celebrated Boer commander, Christiaan de Wet, lamented that it was difficult to sustain operations with men who constantly insisted on going home to see their families. As British pressure mounted, Boer resistance, like resistance to imperial encroachment generally, fragmented into 17,000 or so 'bitter-enders' and the rest. Five thousand Boers served British forces as National Scouts, largely from resentment of burgher domination of Boer society, or to avoid the concentration camps. Even the vaunted Boer mobility was compromised in part by the reluctance to relinquish their wagons, and became a wasting asset as the war reduced the supply of horses and munitions. Some horseless Boers preferred to return home rather than remain as infantrymen in the company of Afrikaners of a lesser sort. The African population was uniformly pro-British, and became more so as the hard-pressed Boers raided African settlements for food. Africans served the British as scouts, intelligence gatherers and teamsters. The British also enjoyed the technological edge: the steam traction engine (tractor) improved supply beyond the railheads, field telephones improved co-ordination and searchlights, initially borrowed from the De Beers diamond mines, bolstered the defence of depots.

From November 1900 when he became commander-in-chief in South Africa, Kitchener adopted a dual strategy of offensive mobility and attrition of the Boer economic and political base, a strategy with which Hoche and Bugeaud, or the Russians in the Caucasus, even Wellesley to a point, would have concurred. The mobile part of the plan consisted of mounting as many as possible of his men to match the mobility of mounted Boer riflemen – indeed, at the close of 'Black Week', Buller had wired for reinforcements drawn from the hunting and shooting classes who could match Boer martial skills. Replicating the beater/hunt line technique used by Hoche in the Vendée, Kitchener etched the veld with lines of galvanized iron blockhouses bound together by barbed wire, and equipped with telegraphs and telephones. What became known as the 'Great Hunt of de Wet' began in January 1901, when columns of mounted men, whose goal was to pin the elusive Boer against the blockhouse and concertina fence line, were stretched out over a front of 160 miles. Kitchener's 'drives' became progressively more elaborate until, by May 1902, 17,000 men, formed into a continuous line, trotted toward a string of blockhouses erected along a railway line. Trains equipped with searchlights shunted back and forth, beams dancing across the darkened veld. But while dramatic, this tactic produced no great confrontations between British hunters and Boer quarry, trapped and desperate to break out. Instead, the game most often ensnared in these 'drives' was cattle, horses and wagons. But the effect was the same, as these formed the accoutrements of Boer survival.

The second element of Kitchener's strategy was equally attritional – the destruction of Boer farms and the removal of Boer women and children to camps where they could not support the commandos. Refugee camps for Boer families displaced by the war had appeared as early as July 1900. However, in December, Kitchener ordered this system expanded to remove Boer civilians from areas where commandos were active. Africans were also moved lest they provide supplies or be impressed for labour by Boer commandos. By 1902, sixty concentration camps housed 116,000 inmates.

Kitchener's concentration camps were merely a British version of a time-tested counter-insurgency method. Chinese officials facing the Nien revolt in the 1850s had ordered local authorities to 'clear the fields and strengthen the walls'. The United States had relied on the reservation as a way to separate out friendly and hostile Amerindians, not always with success. The premise of Gallieni's *tache d'huile* strategy in Tonkin, and later Lyautey's in Morocco, was that friendly natives would settle near French posts for security and prosperity, creating in effect what Vietnam-era American soldiers would call 'free-fire zones'. Kitchener's nomenclature was borrowed directly from Spanish General Weyler's *reconcentrado* policies applied in Cuba from 1896 when 300,000 peasants were ordered into cities and towns to deprive Cuban revolutionaries of a support base. Indeed, at the very moment when Kitchener was being denounced for this inhumane policy in South Africa, American soldiers burned villages and reconcentrated much of the populations of the Abra district of northern Luzon and on the island of Samar.

The military benefits of concentration were significant, although this was not always apparent in the short term. Kitchener made it clear that the primary purpose of the camps was to strike a psychological blow at the enemy: 'There is no doubt the women are keeping up the war and are far more bitter than the men,' he wrote to Roberts. By confining women to camps, he would work on the feelings of the men to get back to their farms. In fact, in the short term the camps may have instilled some discipline in the Boer commandos by liberating their men from the requirement to visit their families and defend their homes, which were now non-existent. In this sense, the concentrations camps were similar to reservations, support systems which freed braves to raid unencumbered by the impedimenta of families. In the long term, however, the concentration of populations does appear to have undermined Boer morale. When the Boers surrendered in May 1902, many cited as their main reason for giving up the struggle the misery of their women and children in the camps.

To be effective, however, the concentration of populations had to meet certain basic conditions. To remove the population from the areas of operation was insufficient by itself to produce strategic results

Kitchener should have been forewarned by the humanitarian outcry over General Weyler's 'concentration' of the Cuban population. Typhoid, measles and dysentery were the constant companions of the 154,000 Boer and African civilians confined to Kitchener's camps, in which at least 20,000 Boers and 12,000 Africans, many of them children, perished.

because this was a purely defensive measure. To succeed, any strategy must have an offensive component. Kitchener's success relied on a combination of the concentration of the enemy population and 'drives' to keep die-hard Boers on the run. For his part, Weyler merely locked himself up in the major provincial towns and left the Cuban revolutionaries free to roam the deserted countryside, and to attack those plantations which still dared to operate. While Weyler's militarily passive and politically repressive policies drove many Cubans into exile or into the arms of the insurgents, Kitchener's 'drives' left no sanctuaries to which Boer civilians seeking to avoid concentration

The second half of Kitchener's population concentration policy was to scorch the earth over which the guerrillas roamed. Here, a Boer farm goes up in flames, at once removing shelter and sustenance as well as striking a blow against insurgent morale.

could flee. In a similar vein, the American Army succeeded in pacifying northern Luzon by 1902 with a combination of the concentration of the populations in the cities and towns, and aggressive strikes against guerrilla bands in the hinterland.

The second requirement for a successful concentration was that it must be part of a hearts-and-minds approach to win support for the incumbent power. Adequate preparations must be made for the care of those evacuated to the camps. This was not always an easy task in marginal agricultural societies, where the army was too busy burning farms and destroying crops to prepare a proper reception for the refugees. The result might be a humanitarian disaster which could jeopardize victory. This is precisely what happened to Kitchener, Weyler, and also to German generals in South-West Africa. Although Joseph Chamberlain defended Kitchener's camps as a humanitarian solution, the results were disastrous. Because of poor preparation, lack of sanitation and shelter, at least 20,000 Boers and 12,000 Africans perished, mostly children under 16 years old. Weyler forced Cuban peasants into towns unprepared to receive the refugees, who perished by the thousands. Horror at the appalling loss of life caused by Weyler's *reconcentrado* was a prime incitement to America's 1898 intervention. In South-West Africa, the Germans confined 17,000 Herero and Nama to camps, almost half of whom perished.

Concentration worked fairly well on Luzon, in part because it was conceived as part of a positive strategy to win the loyalty of the population, rather than simply to remove them from the battlefield. Filipinos were fed, organized into militias, and given a role in municipal government. Like the Chinese officials fighting the Nien, the Americans on Luzon discovered that the principle benefit of militias was less as a defence force, than as a way to filter out disloyal elements. If the population were fed and protected from guerrilla reprisals, it could be induced to surrender its neutrality and support the Americans. If this were not done systematically, then the insurgents might infiltrate the towns and camps to murder or intimidate supporters of the incumbent power, even to create parallel hierarchies, as happened to the French *regroupement* efforts during the Algerian war of 1954–62. American success on Luzon was not replicated on the island of Samar, where American troops destroyed most of the food, and herded the population into towns which could not support them. So desperate did the situation become that starving refugees joined with guerrillas to slaughter the US garrison at Balangiga in September 1901.

Poorly run concentration programmes might prove doubly disastrous for an imperial commander because they provided ammunition for anti-war groups at home. Kitchener's camps became a vehicle through which anti-war groups in Britain attacked the morality of the war. Britain's invasion of the Boer republics had already left it with a public relations problem. Most of the world preferred to see the conflict as a confrontation between a simple farming people victimized by a clique of grasping capitalists, Boer 'Davids' defending hearth and home against the imperial British 'Goliath'. An anti-war demonstration was held in Trafalgar Square on 9 July 1899, three months before war was declared. Irish nationalists, led by the actress Maude Gonne, operating on the assumption that Britain's discomfort was Ireland's opportunity, urged their countrymen to boycott British recruiting stations. But though opposition to the war was concentrated among the working classes and some members of the Liberal Party, the left was by no means unified in its opposition. The Boers also had a bad press because of their shabby treatment of Blacks and of *Uitlanders* (white, mainly British, workers in the diamond and gold mines who faced discrimination by the Boer republics). Vocal opposition to the war in foreign newspapers put the anti-war movement in a delicate position, especially in the wake of 'Black Week'. The journalist W. T. Stead established a 'Stop-the-War' movement, and the Liberal politician Lloyd George used the *Daily News* as a mouthpiece for his anti-war sentiments. Anti-war meetings were held all over Britain in 1900, although patriotic mobs succeeded in disrupting most of them. Their most spectacular success occurred on 18 December 1901 when Lloyd

*Young Welsh politician David Lloyd George,
who came to prominence as a spokesman for the
anti-war movement, almost fell victim to a pro-
war mob in Birmingham in December 1901. The
anti-war movement divided the Liberal Party's
response to the war, while it encouraged
Conservatives to rally round the government.*

George, caught in a mêlée involving over
40,000 people, was forced to flee Birmingham
town hall disguised as a policeman.

Anti-war sentiment declined by the
summer of 1900, as the sieges of Ladysmith
and Mafeking were lifted, the Boer capitals
were seized, and the war disintegrated into an
inconclusive counter-insurgency campaign
whose major victims were women and
children. The Boers had protested the treatment of their families in the
concentration camps almost immediately. But even middle-class British
families were divided over the issue. Some organized or joined groups
which visited the camps or those for Boer POWs on the island of St
Helena. The denunciation of the impact of military action on Boer
civilians by Emily Hobhouse, daughter of a family prominent in
Liberal politics, stirred the War Office to dispatch a committee of
women to investigate conditions in the camps. It also stirred the army
to arrest and expel Hobhouse back to Britain in October 1901, an
action which only allowed her to spread revelations of mass
deportations, burned-out farms, and feverish children. The leader of
the Liberal Party, Sir Henry Campbell-Bannerman, was moved, on
meeting Hobhouse, to denounce 'these methods of barbarism'.

One must not exaggerate the consequences of opposition to the Boer
War – few anti-war MPs were elected, and enlistment in the army
remained high. Nevertheless, the issue of the concentration camps
pointed to one of imperialism's Achilles' heels: the moral ambivalence

of Europeans toward it. This was hardly a new phenomenon. Already in the 1840s, the French public had been outraged when news spread that French soldiers campaigning in the coastal mountains north of Cheliff had made a habit of building fires in the mouths of caves in which Arabs sought refuge, thereby asphyxiating them. Alexis de Tocqueville, who visited Algeria in 1846, wrote that Algerian service had distorted the values of French soldiers, and opened a gulf between European claims to bring civilization and order to the outside world, and the bitter realities of conquest. French imperialism was pursued by scandal. In 1899, Captain Paul Voulet and Lieutenant Charles Chanoine, son of an ex-war minister, murdered their senior officer and led their Senegalese *tirailleurs* and native auxiliaries in mutiny during a campaign against the Mossi States on the upper Volta. 'The events make us blush', the Parisian daily, *Le Temps*, declared, and hardly reflected credit on the French army which at that very moment was in the process of re-trying Captain Alfred Dreyfus for the crime of espionage. It was in part to counter this poor press that Lyautey wrote '*Du rôle coloniale de l'armée*' in the prestigious *Revue des Deux Mondes* in 1900. Lyautey's was an old theme: the army's primary role in the colonies was a social and economic one. 'The colonial soldier was more than a warrior. He was an administrator, farmer, architect and engineer. He sacrificed himself, not for personal gain and glory, but in the cause of developing the economic potential of the colonies.'

No one in France, even on the Left, seriously opposed imperialism. However, they could be counted on to criticize brutalities carried out by the military in the name of spreading Western civilization. The same phenomena could be seen in other countries. Attacks on Amerindian villages by the US Army, even in response to provocation, would often produce howls of protest in the east. While American anti-imperialists denounced the devastation of provinces, the shooting of captives, the torture of prisoners and of unarmed peaceful civilians in the Philippines, their impact was minimal once McKinley defeated anti-imperialist democrat William Jennings Bryant for the presidency in

1900. The brutal repression of the Herero and Maji-Maji rebellions provoked an intense debate over colonial policy in the Reichstag in 1906–7. However, only the Social Democrats advocated abandoning the colonies. Most critics sought merely to tighten Berlin's control over the colonies, and to use the colonial issue as a vehicle for a liberalization of the German political system.

Therefore, the moral issues raised by imperial warfare were insufficient, at least before 1918, to rattle the confidence of imperial nations in their basic right to extend the frontiers of empire against the wishes of the inhabitants. The more important issue flagged first by the Fashoda crisis and subsequently by the Boer War was that of imperial overstretch. The huge military effort required by Britain to defeat a handful of Boer farmers, and the international outcry caused by the war, propelled Britain toward a major re-evaluation of its foreign and defence policies at the turn of the century. But if Britain had bumped into a boulder of resistance in southern Africa, Russian imperialism struck an iceberg in Manchuria.

THE RUSSO-JAPANESE WAR

The greatest collision of rival imperial ambitions occurred not in Africa, but in the Far East. The slow implosion of the Ch'ing (Manchu) dynasty, which was apparent by the conclusion of the Opium War in 1842, if not before, and accelerated in mid century with the Taiping and Nien rebellions, found the Western imperial powers circling vulture-like over the decomposing carcass of China. Most were content to carve out spheres of influence, coastal enclaves from which they could pursue trade and maintain pressure on Beijing. However, two powers, Japan and Russia, nurtured territorial ambitions on the Asian mainland. Russia's collision with Japan over Manchuria and Korea produced the most devastating imperial war, one which topped in destruction and casualties all the colonial conflagrations hitherto fought. The Russo-Japanese War of 1904–5 offered a desolate preview of the war Europe was to experience between 1914 and 1918.

At the turn of the century Japan contained a contradiction. Although the Meiji Restoration of 1868 was initiated in reaction to Western imperialism, Japan succumbed to imperialism to the point that the success of reform was measured in great part by the status which Japan gained through expansion on to the Asian mainland. Meiji reformers believed that an aggressive foreign policy offered the best vehicle to build consensus for reform at home. From the 1860s, they argued that a forward policy in Korea would instantly change Japan's outmoded customs, set its objectives abroad, promote its industry and technology, and eliminate jealousy and recrimination among its people. Foreign policy was an extension of domestic consolidation. By 1876, Japan had begun to imitate Western-style gunboat diplomacy in Korea, a Chinese vassal state, as a pre-requisite to establishing Japanese economic, political and military influence over the peninsula. This divided Korea, and caused conservatives close to the Korean court to appeal to China as a protector. In 1885, China and Japan agreed to keep their troops out of Korea. But when the Chinese sent soldiers to crush a rebellion there in 1894, Tokyo cried foul. In July, Japan landed troops in Korea, Liaotung and Shantung. The Sino-Japanese War succeeded beyond Tokyo's wildest dreams. By March 1895 Japan had captured Port Arthur, Darien and destroyed most of the Chinese fleet. The Japanese population was ecstatic. Japan demanded a large indemnity, most-favoured nation status, and the opening of treaty ports. The army occupied Liaotung, while the navy seized Taiwan. But hardly was the ink dry on the treaty that ended the Sino-Japanese War than Germany, France and Russia intervened in order to force Japan to give up Liaotung.

This big power intervention was a setback. But Tokyo vowed to make it only a temporary one. Industrialization, the growth of trade with China and of the merchant navy was seen as synonymous with imperial expansion. The American takeover of the Philippines from 1898, and the Boxer Rebellion of 1900, increased pressure on Japan to act before it had little room left for manoeuvre. In 1901 Japan became one of the

A March 1904 Japanese characterization of Russian imperialism as a black octopus, one of whose tentacles lay across Port Arthur and the Liaotung Peninsula that Japan had occupied but had been forced by Germany, France and Russia to surrender at the end of the Sino-Japanese War of 1894–5.

Boxer Protocol Powers, with the right to station troops in Peking-Tientsin. The following year, it signed a treaty with Britain, making Tokyo London's principal partner in Asia. But Tokyo continued to view control of the Korean Peninsula as vital for its defence. It tried to negotiate an exchange of Korea for Manchuria with Russia, but St Petersburg turned a deaf ear. Indeed, Japan's clumsy policies there, which included the murder of Queen Min, only drove the Koreans into the arms of the Russians. Tokyo increasingly came to the view that the only way to defend its aspirations to great power status, to settle the Manchurian question, and to consolidate its power base at home was to pick a fight with Russia. If the risks of defeat were great, the risks of doing nothing were marginalization abroad, the failure of reform at home, and a return to the anarchy and civil wars of the Shogun era.

Like Japan, Russia was enticed into the Far East by the slow implosion of China. However, unlike Japan which saw imperialism as the centerpiece of Meiji reform, Russia's imperial enterprise was unreflective. Russian gunboats had been on the Amur river, which separated Siberia

China, foreign presence, foreign attack and Chinese reactions 1894–1900

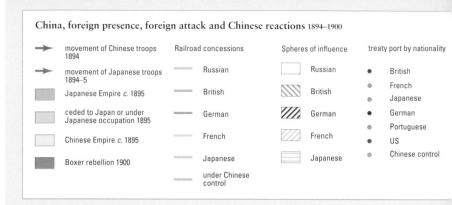

→ movement of Chinese troops 1894	Railroad concessions	Spheres of influence	treaty port by nationality
→ movement of Japanese troops 1894–5	═══ Russian	▢ Russian	● British
▢ Japanese Empire c. 1895	═══ British	▨ British	◉ French
			◉ Japanese
▢ ceded to Japan or under Japanese occupation 1895	═══ German	▨ German	● German
			◉ Portuguese
▢ Chinese Empire c. 1895	─── French	▨ French	● US
▧ Boxer rebellion 1900	─── Japanese	▤ Japanese	◉ Chinese control
	─── under Chinese control		

THE SINO-JAPANESE WAR, 1894–5

By the 1890s regional and religious insurgencies, foreign bullying, failed reform movements, and nascent warlordism had seriously undermined the authority of the Ch'ing dynasty. Manoeuvres by Tokyo and St Petersburg to capitalize on Chinese weakness brought them into conflict over Manchuria and Korea.

from Manchuria, since the 1850s. In 1875, Russia had recognized Japanese suzerainty over the Kurile Islands in exchange for Russian ownership of Sakhalin. Russian officers had arrived in Korea as military instructors in the 1880s. But Russian interest in the Far East was only stimulated when Japan seized the Liaotung Peninsula in 1894. Nicholas II appears to have nurtured the belief that Russia would become an Asian power. Japan's rapid defeat of China raised the fears that Tokyo would pre-empt that dream. The Russian foreign minister argued that Tokyo was merely acting as London's agent. Vladivostok was imperilled. The tsar's finance minister, Sergei Witte, insisted that vast profits awaited the nation that exploited Manchuria and China. These profits, Witte argued, could be re-invested in Russian industrial development.

No one in St Petersburg thought through the strategic consequences when, in 1895, Russia posed as China's benefactor and orchestrated the international pressure which filched from Japan many of the spoils of its victory over China. Russia's reward from Beijing was permission to

direct the Trans-Siberian Railway across Manchuria as a shortcut to
Vladivostok. The presence of the railway allowed Russian railway
police to patrol the Manchurian lines and, in 1898, to annex the
Liaotung Peninsula with its two important ports, Port Arthur and
Dalny. Following the Boxer Rebellion of 1900, Russia brought its
military occupation of Manchuria into the open to guarantee China's
good behaviour, and sent forestry workers into Korea. But Russia's
trade deficit with China grew, and, as both army and navy leaders
pointed out, it lacked the manpower to defend these far-flung outposts.
Russia also seemed blind to the foreign policy consequences of its Far

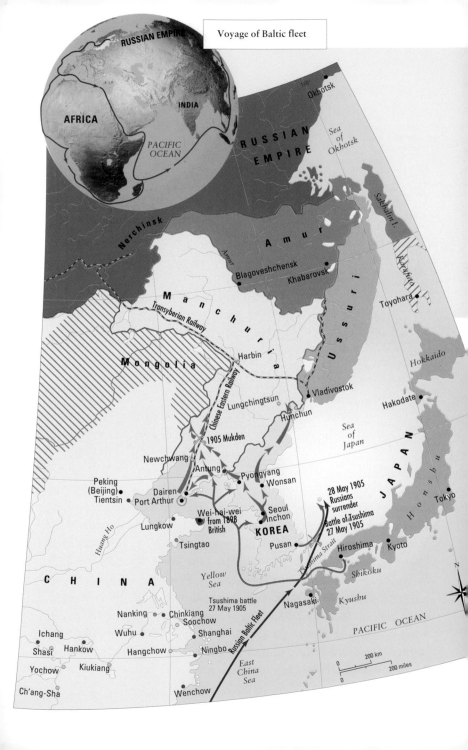

Voyage of Baltic fleet

RUSSIAN EMPIRE

AFRICA

INDIA

PACIFIC
OCEAN

Okhotsk

Sea
of
Okhotsk

R U S S I A N

E M P I R E

Nerchinsk

Amur

Sakhalin I.

Blagoveshchensk

Khabarovsk

M a n c h u r i a

U s s u r i

Transyberian Railway

Toyohara

Kurile Is.

Hokkaido

Harbin

Mongolia

Chinese Eastern Railway

Lungchingtsun

Vladivostok

Hakodate

Hunchun

Sea
of
Japan

1905 Mukden

J A P A N

Newchwang

Antung

Pyongyang

Wonsan

Peking
(Beijing)

Dairen

Tientsin

Port Arthur

Wei-hai-wei
from 1898
British

Seoul

Inchon

28 May 1905
Russians
surrender

Battle of Tsushima
27 May 1905

H o n s h u

Tokyo

Lungkow

KOREA

Huang Ho

Tsingtao

Pusan

Hiroshima

Kyoto

C H I N A

Yellow
Sea

Tsushima battle
27 May 1905

Tsushima Strait

Shikoku

Nanking

Chinkiang
Soochow

Nagasaki

Kyushu

PACIFIC   OCEAN

Ichang

Wuhu

Shanghai

Hankow

Hangchow

Ningbo

Russian Baltic Fleet

Shasi

East
China
Sea

0   200 km

Yochow

Kiukiang

0   200 miles

Ch'ang-Sha

Wenchow

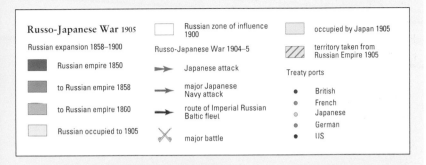

THE RUSSO-JAPANESE WAR, 1904–5

Japan took a huge risk in attacking Russia. But Tokyo concluded that inaction would result in Japan's marginalization and the collapse of the Meiji experiment. Japan's principal strategic advantage lay in sea control.

Eastern deployment – both the Anglo-Japanese Alliance of 1902 and the open door policy declared by the United States were attempts to check Russian expansion into China.

But it was Japan which felt most threatened. After Russia refused to reassure Japan that it harboured no ambitions in Korea, Japan broke off diplomatic relations on 5 February 1904. Three days later, on the night of 8/9 February, Admiral Togo sent his torpedo boats against the Russian Pacific squadron anchored at Port Arthur. The destruction of the Pacific squadron was a vital objective for the Japanese. Russian ships operating out of Port Arthur could threaten the sea lines of communication between the Japanese islands and Japanese troops on the mainland. Also, if Russia decided to dispatch its Baltic fleet to the Pacific (the Black Sea fleet was prohibited passage through the Bosphorus), Togo's ships would be desperately outnumbered and outgunned in the ensuing main fleet action. But poor intelligence, faulty tactics and Togo's desire to preserve his cruisers, which might have finished off the cornered Russian squadron, meant that only three Russian ships were damaged in the surprise attack. Nevertheless, Russian naval commanders were unable to profit from their escape. Their tactics were equally timid, especially after sorties into the Pacific ended in encounters with mines. The naval war before Port Arthur settled into a temporary stalemate, as the Russians seemed content to await the arrival of their Baltic fleet.

Stymied on the sea, the Japanese were forced to attack the Pacific squadron from the land side. Troops were landed at Chemulpo and broke through Russian defences on the Yalu river. This Japanese victory was celebrated as the first victory of Asians over Western forces,

Japanese troops land in Korea in 1904. Russian forces made only an ineffectual effort to defend Manchuria on the Yalu, and instead retreated to Port Arthur where they were besieged.

although Chinese troops had defeated the French at Lang Son and checked the French invasion of Formosa in 1885. Japanese forces moved north toward Liaoyang to cut the railway line leading down to Port Arthur. Meanwhile, Japanese soldiers landed at Pi-tzu-wo and moved toward Nanshan, a narrow isthmus which controls the entrance to the Liaotung Peninsula and Port Arthur. The Russian defences were not well sited, and only 4,000 Russians manned them against 35,000 Japanese troops supported by naval artillery. None the less, Russian machine guns ripped the close ranks of attacking Japanese troops to shreds.

By the end of the day, it looked as if the Russian position on the isthmus would hold, when Japanese soldiers, aided by naval bombardment, gained a toehold on the western flank of the Russian line. The Russian General Fock ordered a general retreat which turned into a panic. The Japanese moved south to capture Dalny. Thanks mainly to the inaction of the Russian Pacific squadron, Dalny became a major support base for the siege of Port Arthur.

The conflict settled into a war of attrition, battles fought between armies that numbered tens of thousands of men, backed by artillery and machine guns. Time seemed to be on Russia's side. Its resources in men and *matériel* were potentially immense, while those of the Japanese were limited. Although Japan could get its troops to the front by sea faster than Russia could move their soldiers the 5,500 miles over the single-track Trans-Siberian Railway, Russian engineers began to add track. Russia also ordered its Baltic fleet to the Far East. But St Petersburg failed to make time work for them. The Russian commander, Kuropatkin, wanted to delay operations until the Trans-Siberian Railway could ensure the delivery of reinforcements. But St Petersburg, fearing the fall of Port Arthur and with it the end of the Pacific squadron, pressured their commanders into battles they preferred for the moment to avoid. Russian ground forces were poorly led. They continually abandoned strong positions because their commanders lost their nerve. Although Russian use of artillery was good, ground forces remained on the tactical defensive, lacked initiative, and failed to counter-attack when the Japanese were exhausted and over-extended. The naval forces at Port Arthur and Vladivostok were also largely passive, when they might have helped their armies by attacking Japanese sea communications with the home islands.

The Japanese, meanwhile, sought to force a decision before Russia could mobilize the full force of its strength against them. Their plan was quickly to seize Port Arthur, thus eliminating the Pacific squadron, then turn north and inflict decisive defeats on the Russians before their reinforcements could arrive. The Japanese absorbed huge casualties in desperate and unimaginative frontal assaults against Russian positions at Liaoyang in August 1904, and at Sha ho, before Mukden, in October.

Admiral Togo's surprise attack on the Russian Pacific squadron at Port Arthur on the night of 8–9 February, 1904 aimed to prevent Russian ships from impeding Japanese sea lanes of communication. The attack failed to neutralize the Russian squadron, which meant that Port Arthur had to be taken, at great cost, by the army.

Port Arthur surrendered in January 1905, but the carnage had been horrific. The Japanese had suffered 60,000 casualties in the siege of the port – 8,000 alone in the eight-day attempt to seize 204-metre hill – to about half that many for the defenders. The depressing irony for Tokyo was that Japanese forces had taken Port Arthur from the Chinese in 1894 at the cost of sixteen soldiers. A Russian counter-offensive south of Mukden at Sandepu in January 1905 got them nowhere, but cost another 14,000 men. The final major land battle of the war occurred at Mukden in February. The battle lasted three weeks, was fought along a front of 100 miles, and cost the Russians 61,000 casualties to 41,000 for the Japanese.

Japanese artillerymen load a 500-pound shell into one of eighteen huge Japanese coastal defence guns (called 'Osaka Babies' after the town where they were made), mustered to pound Port Arthur into submission.

The final straw for the Russians came when their Baltic fleet under Admiral Rozhdestvenskii limped into the Korean Straits on 28 May, only to have his T twice crossed by Admiral Togo; this allowed the Japanese to fire their guns broadside at the Russian ships, which could only reply with their forward turrets. The battle of Tsushima was a

The battle of Tsushima, 27–28 May 1905, was hailed by sea-power enthusiasts as the decisive battle of the war, the event that caused the tsar to opt for peace. But other factors such as mutinies in his forces, strikes that disrupted the Trans-Siberian Railway, and fear of an attack from Germany were at least as influential in the tsar's decision.

disastrous end to a long and demoralizing voyage. Only three ships of the Baltic fleet reached Vladivostok. The Russian decision to negotiate came just in the nick of time for Tokyo, which was broke, racked by inflation, and just about out of troops. Russian intelligence reported Japanese distress to the tsar. But Nicholas decided to throw in the towel. His fleet lay at the bottom of the Pacific, and his sailors had mutinied at Vladivostok, Sevastopol and Kronstadt in sympathy with the strikes which had erupted across Russia and disrupted the Trans-Siberian Railway. Russia's major ally, France, urged him to cut his losses. He was also worried that the need to send soldiers to the East had denuded his European defences. Peace was signed at Portsmouth, New Hampshire, on 5 September 1905.

With victory in the Russo-Japanese War, Japan had achieved the status of a great power and joined the ranks of imperial powers. It annexed Korea as a colony in 1910. The collapse of the Ch'ing (Manchu) dynasty in 1912 and the outbreak of the First World War two years later, which caused the retreat of the Western powers toward Europe, cleared the way for Japan's aggressive imperialism in the Far East. But if Japan could replicate the success of the Western imperial powers, it could also duplicate their errors. Japan's search for security in imperial expansion would only produce insecurity, isolation, alienation and over-extension as it collided with the rising nationalism of China and Korea, and eventually with the Pacific interests of the United States.

THE CONQUEST OF MOROCCO

Japan's desire for recognition of its great power status in the Far East was matched in Europe by Germany, which moved to thwart French ambitions in Morocco. On the morning of 31 March 1905, the German liner Hamburg swung at anchor off Tangier. On board, the kaiser stared across the grey water, whipped to foam by a persistent force 8 gale, and debated whether to land. At about 11.30 in the morning he re-emerged on deck dressed in a field uniform of the Prussian Army –

silver helmet with chinstrap, polished black boots, red gloves, a revolver attached to a cord which hung around his neck and a sabre dangling at his side – was lowered into a whaler, and rowed past two French cruisers, the *Du Chayla* and the *Linois*, towards the shore. Two large German sailors plucked him from the boat and carried him the last few yards to the wooden steps which he mounted to the quay. The visitor said something in German to the representative of the sultan of Morocco, Abd el-Malek, who greeted him. But as Abd el-Malek spoke no German, and as the kaiser's remarks were inaudible to others, what the kaiser actually said remains a mystery. The German was hoisted on to a horse and, his semi-paralysed arm dangling by his side, led through a hedge of French marines stiff at present arms, and Moroccan askars who approximated a similar salute. The party plunged into the narrow streets of Tangier which French residents, with the encouragement of their legation, had festooned in red, white and blue bunting. They processed through the Grand Soko where savage-looking Rif tribesmen shouted and discharged their muskets and pitched them into the air in welcome, to emerge at the German consulate where the town's diplomats had sought refuge from the morning's pelting rain. The kaiser entered the building, muttered some homilies about respecting the interests of German commerce, made his way back to the shore and sailed away, faintly pursued by the beating of drums and the ululations of the Moroccan women. The next day, the German consul in Tangier, Richard von Kuhlmann, announced that the kaiser's visit had been intended to underscore Germany's commitment to Morocco's continued independence.

The German declaration stunned both London and Paris, as much as it delighted the Moroccans. It also represented a bold, even a foolhardy, diplomatic move on the part of Berlin. By replacing Britain as the guarantor of Moroccan independence, Germany had declared the Entente Cordiale dead, or so Berlin thought. In 1904, Britain had bartered Moroccan independence against overdue French acquiescence to the British domination of Egypt. In seeking an accommodation with

Britain, French colonialists reasoned from an Algerian perspective. Although the last serious uprising in Algeria had occurred in 1871 while the French army was otherwise occupied fighting the Franco-Prussian war, the French felt desperately insecure there. In 1881, France had absorbed Tunisia, thereby guaranteeing the safety of Algeria's eastern borders. In the west, however, Morocco remained turbulent and unstable, a fireship on the flank of Algeria. The Entente Cordiale also had a European dimension, although in 1904 it was a latent one. The French foreign minister, Théophile Delcassé, eager for British friendship to counterbalance an increasingly powerful and assertive Germany, sought to end what in his view was a needless and destructive imperial rivalry between two countries who otherwise had no real conflicts of interest.

German reasons for challenging the Entente Cordiale were complex. The long-term causes resided in the vague longing for a recognition of Germany's international status which equalled Berlin's economic and military power. Kaiser Wilhelm II headed a gaggle of parvenu

Kaiser Wilhelm visits Tangier in 1905 to emphasize Germany's support for continued Moroccan independence. This clumsy attempt to crack the Anglo-French entente of 1904, according to which Britain recognized French suzerainty in Morocco in return for acknowledgement of British dominion in Egypt, drove the two erstwhile imperial rivals closer together.

politicians and military men desperate for respect from the older, established powers. The German chancellor, Prince von Bülow, complained that France, Britain and Russia refused to 'recognize our dignity and our recently acquired authority as a world power'. Much of this was for home consumption. By playing the nationalist card the German leadership was merely aping governments elsewhere in Europe. Status in turn-of-the-century Europe was measured, at least in part, by the dimensions of one's colonial empire. Unfortunately for Germany, most of the territory available for colonization had already been snatched by Britain and France, to a large extent because Bismarck had shown so little interest in empire building. Morocco remained, however, and it was on this hapless land that this new generation of German leaders adjusted their sights.

The short-term causes of what became known as the 'Tangier crisis' resided in the equally ill-fated attempt on the part of von Bülow to isolate France diplomatically. France's major ally, Russia, was already engaged in a catastrophic war with Japan. If Germany supported Moroccan independence, the German chancellor calculated, Britain would back off from her alliance with France. It was a neat plan, but it contained at least one fallacy – it assumed that Britain would desert her new ally. This was unlikely. For the British, the Fashoda crisis followed by the Second South African War had demonstrated all too painfully how friendless Britain was in the world. The German naval laws of 1898 and 1900, which were a direct challenge to British mastery of the seas, drove this point forcefully home. By 1904, Britain had found her friend in Europe. She intended to stick by her. The Tangier crisis of 1905 was the first step in transforming the colonial *entente* of 1904 into the European military alliance of 1914.

At the best of times, Morocco would be a difficult country to conquer. The land was vast, much of it mountain or semi-desert, all of it remote. Its inhabitants were fiercely independent, although as elsewhere, opposition to the French was spasmodic and unsustained. The greatest risk to the French was that an invasion might provoke a

German reaction. Twice, in 1905 and again in 1911, French encroachments into Morocco brought Berlin and Paris to the very brink of war. Aware of the delicate political situation, General Hubert Lyautey digested eastern Morocco, moving forward by stealth from Algeria to occupy sites within the territory claimed, but not occupied, by the sultan, renaming the villages to throw journalists, diplomats and politicians off the scent. In 1907, the French placed a large force ashore at Casablanca after Europeans were massacred there, and pursued the conquest of the Chaouia, the hinterland behind the city. Moroccan

Colonel Charles Mangin greets the new French Resident General of Morocco, General Hubert Lyautey, at the gates of Marrakesh in 1912. Lyautey instructed Mangin to seize Marrakesh despite strict orders from Paris to the contrary.

tribesmen mounted a briefly effective mobile campaign against the French columns sent out from Casablanca. However, resistance largely collapsed in March 1908 after French General Albert d'Amade twice caught the resisters in their camps against which he brought the full power of French artillery and small arms.

In eastern Morocco in that year, Lyautey provoked an uprising of the Beni Snassen when French forces occupied Oudjda on the Algerian frontier. A *harka*, or war party, numbering perhaps 4,000 men, imprudently attacked up a narrow ravine against a concentration of French forces on the Wadi Kiss and was decimated by artillery. A second *harka* attempted to take Port Say on the Mediterranean coast and was driven off by naval gunfire. A third *harka* surprised a French camp at Mennaba in eastern Morocco at dawn on 17 April 1908. But despite initial success they fell to looting, which allowed the more disciplined French forces to counter-attack. Final battles occurred in May at Bou Denib, and in September at Djorf, where the Moroccans again foolishly massed against French artillery and machine-guns and were slaughtered in great numbers. The final French push into Morocco was precipitated in 1911 by a mutiny of the sultan's *askars* against their French advisers in Fez. A French expedition launched to rescue the Europeans and the sultan besieged there touched off an international crisis which was only extinguished in November 1911, when the French won the freedom to act in Morocco by giving the Germans territorial concessions in the Cameroon.

The conquest of Morocco underscored the rising costs to France, both diplomatic and military, of imperial warfare. If the 1911 accord settled the Moroccan question, it was only the beginning of France's attempt to impose its control over the country, the last corner of which did not submit until 1934. In the aftermath of the Franco-Prussian War of 1870–71, the French Army counted 15,300 white and 7,420 indigenous troops in its colonial forces, including those stationed in Algeria. The rebellion against the French takeover of Tunisia had caused Paris to dispatch 35,000 troops from France in July 1881, most of whom had to be quickly withdrawn because of disease, and replaced by Algerian units. The French invasion of Tonkin began with 4,000 troops in 1883, and swelled in the face of Chinese intervention and popular resistance to 40,000 by 1885. The Madagascar campaign of 1895 required around 15,000 officers and men. Most of the expeditions in sub-Saharan African could be accomplished with less than 3,000 men (Dodds took 3,400 to Dahomey in 1892), in part because it was difficult to support larger numbers logistically, but also because enemy resistance was seldom overwhelming. The Fashoda crisis so stretched military resources that in 1898 the army violated French law to place over 12,000 metropolitan conscripts in the colonial forces. The 60,000 troops dispatched to deal with the crisis of 1911 made Morocco the most costly of all French imperial expeditions. The French intervention there came at a particularly bad time, for it brought an unwanted financial burden at the very moment when the government added a third year of conscript service to match an increase in German army strength. The costs of Morocco also complicated plans to add heavy artillery to the army's arsenal. The French commander-in-chief, General Joseph Joffre, feared that the Moroccan expedition would compromise French mobilization for war against Germany. By the outbreak of the First World War, 42,100 white and 88,108 native troops were drawing rations in the colonies or France. The French maintained the equivalent of two army corps to garrison Algeria before 1914. The great cost of occupying the colonies fuelled the debate between colonialists like General Charles Mangin, who argued in his 1910 book, *La force noire,* that the colonies offered inexhaustible repositories of manpower to defend the homeland, and others, like Georges Clemenceau, who insisted that colonial expansion subtracted military strength from the vital north-eastern frontier with Germany. Ironically, it was Clemenceau who, as prime minister from 1917, proved most willing to mobilize colonial manpower to defend France. Therefore, the greatest benefit of colonies for France was the million and a half subjects they sent to support the French war effort between 1914 and 1918.

CHAPTER FIVE

Imperial Twilight?

Members of the Algerian Front de Liberation National pose before Second World War surplus British Lewis machine guns in 1957. The FLN became adept at setting helicopter ambushes during the Algerian War of 1954–62.

Imperial Twilight?

After 1918, the perception of imperial warfare held by the colonialists gradually altered, for reasons that had more to do with events in Europe than with those in the colonies. In Callwell's day, imperial conquest had come to be seen merely as a technical problem to be mastered by the application of a fairly predictable mixture of organization, technology, and tactical élan. Following the First World War, however, imperial warfare was gradually transformed in the minds of Europeans into an almost unstoppable force, a revolution nourished by social resentment, economic oppression and nationalist fervour. An indication of how much the perception of warfare outside Europe had been altered by the First World War is apparent in the 1929 edition of the *Encyclopaedia Britannica*. Although C. E. Callwell had contributed articles to the *Britannica*, the author chosen for the entry on 'Guerrilla Warfare' was not Callwell, but T. E. Lawrence. In a mere four pages, the hero of the Arab Revolt offered a vision of small wars which appeared to consign the 559 pages of Callwell's 1906 text, as well as a century's experience in imperial warfare, to oblivion. Lawrence wrote: 'Here is the thesis: given mobility, security [in the

The success of the 'Arab Revolt' against the Turks in the First World War, and the public's romantic fascination with its chief propagandist, T. E. Lawrence, announced the revival of insurgency as a potent form of warfare. In fact, the Arab success replicated that of Spanish guerrillas during the Peninsular War, rather than announce a new insurgent era.

form of denying targets to the enemy], time, and doctrine [the idea to convert every subject to friendliness], victory will rest with the insurgents, for the algebraical factors are in the end decisive, and against them the perfections of means and spirit struggle quite in vain.'

Lawrence's praise of the potency of insurgent movements is somewhat puzzling, because it is grounded in little hard evidence. A century and a half of imperial warfare had produced some notable insurgent successes. Many of the colonies of North and South American had gained independence through clever strategies that denied targets to the enemy. Ideologies of nationalism had united significant portions of the population, while foreign intervention had both imported military skills and, in the case of French intervention in the American Revolution, over-extended the incumbent power. Mexico's success against the French in 1867 relied on a similar combination of factors. Afghanistan had been invaded, and abandoned, because it was wild, remote, and of little strategic interest once the British acknowledged Russia's indifference to the place. Abyssinian independence was preserved at Adowa because successful tactical adaptations to the firearm coincided with remarkable incompetence on the part of the Italians. The United States intervened in 1898 to break the stalemate between rebels and Spanish forces in Cuba. But the list of failed resistance to Western encroachment was more extensive by far than this brief catalogue of successes. Over the course of the eighteenth and nineteenth centuries, a mere handful of Western soldiers and their indigenous allies had managed to conquer Africa, India and much of Asia.

Did the insurgent balance sheet change all that much between 1918 and the outbreak of the Second World War? In 1921, the southern counties of Ireland had shed their colonial status, at least in part through military means. But interwar imperial rebellions in India, the Levant and Morocco were crushed. Even Mao Tse-tung, regarded as the most sophisticated theorist of modern revolutionary warfare, was notably unsuccessful when he attempted to put his theories into

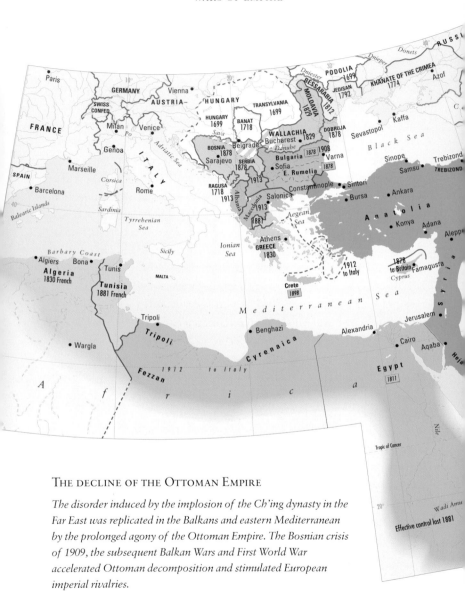

The decline of the Ottoman Empire

The disorder induced by the implosion of the Ch'ing dynasty in the Far East was replicated in the Balkans and eastern Mediterranean by the prolonged agony of the Ottoman Empire. The Bosnian crisis of 1909, the subsequent Balkan Wars and First World War accelerated Ottoman decomposition and stimulated European imperial rivalries.

practice in China in the 1930s. Indeed, Mao may only have become a footnote in history had not Japanese intervention in China prevented Chiang from finishing off the Chinese Communist movement when it was weakened after the Long March of 1935. Lawrence, of course, had played midwife to the Arab Revolt against the Turks during the First World War. But even Lawrence might be forced to concede that Arab success relied on many of the same contingent circumstances that brought victory to Spanish guerrillas who fought Napoleon's armies between 1808 and 1812. Like the Arabs, Spanish insurgents were aided by an outside army that prevented the occupying force from concentrating its full energies against them. Nor does Lawrence explain how an insurgency whose end result was the replacement of Turkish imperialism with French and British rule can be called a victory for the rebellion.

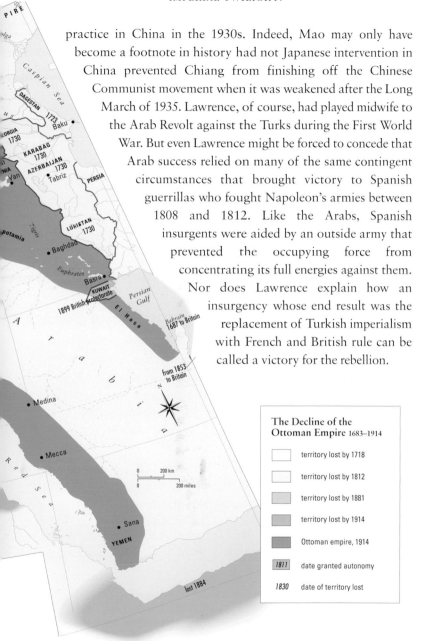

The Decline of the
Ottoman Empire 1683–1914

	territory lost by 1718
	territory lost by 1812
	territory lost by 1881
	territory lost by 1914
	Ottoman empire, 1914
1811	date granted autonomy
1830	date of territory lost

If an increase in insurgent victories does not explain Lawrence's assertion, how can one account for it? Although the era of imperial conquest was a successful one for Western armies, its achievement contained at least three reasons for its ultimate demise after 1918. First, before 1914, native resistance was fragmented because it lacked a common ideology or sense of self-interest. If the regions that fell under imperial domination could conjure up a national consciousness, a sense of identity which eradicated the seams of race, language, religion, caste and custom, then they might articulate a coherent ideological and political response to outside domination. As has been seen, the British colonies of North America, the Spanish colonies of South America, Saint Domingue and, to a certain extent, Mexico between 1862 and 1867 had succeeded in doing this. But these were offshoots of Western imperialism and so could use the ideology and rhetoric of the West in their own defence. Few non-Western societies before the First World War had been able to replicate the success of Meiji Japan, to evolve an adaptive response which allowed them to modernize within the context of their own culture and traditions. Elsewhere, the very tradition which those resisting sought to protect caused them to reject as alien to their culture the modernization they required to defend it. The Chinese attempt to adapt to the Western imperial challenge within the confines of Confucian norms merely produced defeat and disintegration. The same reactionary character coloured resistance movements founded on Islamic precepts. Elsewhere tribalism, and religious and ethnic fragmentation made resistance to imperial encroachment seem nostalgic, even reactionary, which doomed even the most spectacular resistance (such as the Indian Mutiny) to defeat.

It was precisely the beginnings of a process through which indigenous societies acquired the ideological framework for a more efficient adaptive response that Lawrence had observed, and upon which his military reputation was constructed. Lawrence was asked to write about guerrilla warfare, which is a tactic. His insistence that guerrilla warfare was inevitably successful was rooted in his belief that indigenous societies had discovered the ideological counter to imperialism, one that allowed them to achieve the unity which had earlier eluded them. In short, imperialism, in its desire to improve the native, to raise him to Western levels of civilization, bore the germs of its own, if not destruction, at least modification and evolution. Imperial rule was denounced as a triumph of arrogance and racism. The efficiency of Western rule translated into discrimination and oppression, justice into a trespass upon local custom and tradition, economic progress into exploitation, security into wasteful expeditions, forced conscription and, on the margins, atrocity. Imperial schools

Mao Tse-tung in 1935. Mao is regarded as one of the chief theorists and most successful practitioners of insurgency, both on the tactical level, and as a strategy of popular mobilization. Mao broke with other Communist theorists by insisting that revolution should be fomented among the peasants, not in the towns.

which espoused the virtues of citizenship and the 'rights of man' were at odds with the realities of the inferior status of colonial élites which they aimed to educate. The experience of living under and serving in imperial administrations, even in European armies, would generate the national consciousness hitherto conspicuously lacking. This rising national consciousness reduced the divisions and apathy which allowed colonial powers to rule. It also diminished the ability to recruit native

The French Empire 1914

European empires proved to be remarkably fragile creations. The French Empire, though second in size only to Britain's, was in reality an expression of national weakness. It was justified by French officers reacting to the emergence of Germany as a powerful rival in Europe, and was retained as a symbol of status in a world in which French culture, language and influence were in decline. Furthermore, France lacked the power, and the French people the will, to defend the empire against post-Second World War challenges in Indo-China and North Africa.

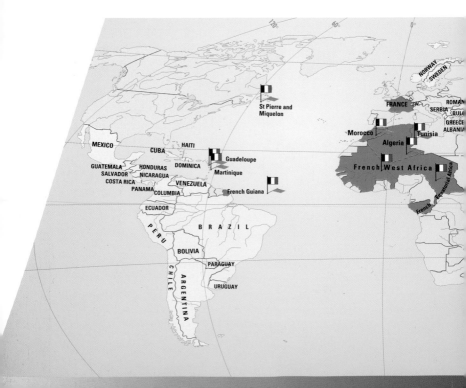

soldiers, and diminished the combative qualities of those native soldiers who still consented to serve the outside power. To this, one might add an overlay of Marxist ideology – another imperial import – which articulated an analytical framework for anti-colonial resistance. In the writings of Mao Tse-tung, some insurgent movements discovered a blueprint for revolution.

Second, with the possible exceptions of Russia and Japan, imperial powers were poorly placed to respond to this emerging nationalism. Russian imperialism was tied closely with Continental security. Russian imperial boundaries had been fleshed out with settlers transplanted to the conquered lands. In Soviet Marxism, Russian imperialism acquired an ideology which papered over, at least temporarily, the cracks in a vast and diverse empire. Russia's decolonization crisis was delayed until the collapse of the Soviet Union, when scores of Russians who had settled in the colonies clamoured for rescue. A fundamental premise of

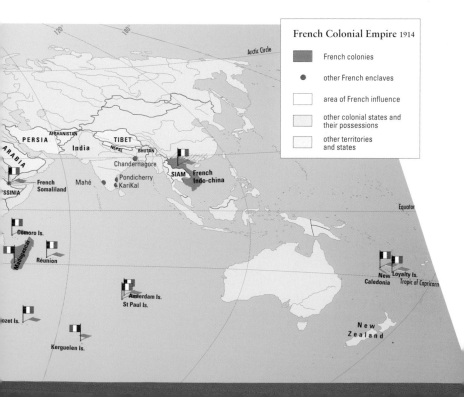

French Colonial Empire 1914

- French colonies
- other French enclaves
- area of French influence
- other colonial states and their possessions
- other territories and states

the Meiji Restoration was that reform, and hence security from Western imperialism, was linked to the imperial domination of Korea and economic and military control of Formosa and northern China. Japan developed an anti-imperialism to counter the Western imperial influence in the Far East, and to co-opt local nationalism in places like the Dutch East Indies for the benefit of Japanese imperialism.

THE DEMISE OF IMPERIALISM

Elsewhere, however, imperialism had never enjoyed widespread popular support even in its high renaissance. At home, imperial expansion brought the risks of strategic over-extension, political unpopularity, economic costs, military defeat, and moral compromise. By the time of the Second South African War, if not before, even the British had begun to realize that Western values which combined moral suasion with the idea of progress were not everywhere exportable. Although outwardly the most successful, certainly the most stylish, imperialists, the British seemed to have wearied of imperialism's responsibilities even as they shouldered them, lost faith in its mission even as they preached its virtues, tired of its wars even as they fought them. Its benefits were largely intangible, limited to the ephemeral satisfaction of painting large areas of the map pink, blue, yellow or whatever colour was chosen to denote the greater Fatherland.

Imperialism in its Gallic manifestation proved more resilient, but hardly bulletproof. Imperial governance adapted more easily to France's authoritarian political culture, where the citizen is considered a moral adolescent in constant need of control and tutelage by a wise administration. French humanitarians might denounce colonial atrocities. But it never occurred to them – at least not in the pre-Marxist era – that imperial peoples should be permitted to forego the opportunity of becoming or remaining part of the French empire simply because they had other priorities. Also, France's vision of national grandeur made imperialism very much a defensive response by a nation and a culture in relative decline in the nineteenth and twentieth

Ironically, two of the most enduring imperial legacies were indigenous nationalism and Marxism. Ho Chi Minh took advantage of resentment over French rule, the vacuum created by the Japanese occupation of Indo-China in the Second World War, and the Japanese surrender in August 1945 to seize power in Hanoi.

centuries. With over 1.5 million colonial subjects contributing to the French war effort between 1914 and 1918, France could rightly conclude that the empire was a force multiplier vital to bolster France's relatively precarious position in Europe. Imperialism was also about insuring France's influence in the world. France's *mission civilizatrice* was the organized export of French language and culture, French influence and, above all, French control. Nevertheless, growing agitation for increased political rights, especially in North Africa and Indo-China, cast a shadow over the future of empire. Challenged by Kipling to take up the 'White Man's Burden', Americans were never more than contrite imperialists. American empire as a formal creation was an unintended consequence of victory in a war with Spain. The dominion over the Philippines was rationalized as a naval base to secure trade routes to the Far East. The islands were pledged independence at the first opportunity.

The final reason for imperialism's demise involved the changing perception of imperial warfare. From a military perspective, imperial warfare came to be seen as a fleeting problem as Europe entered an age of total war. Armies neglected to study a subject so remote from 'real war'. Two world wars largely destroyed the officer corps that had specialized in colonial service, and with them went the expertise, the corporate memory required to fight what travelled under the euphemism of 'low-intensity conflict'. As in the earlier era of imperial conquest, Western armies of the twentieth centuries would prove slow to adapt to the challenges of unconventional war. There was always the temptation to approach non-Western warfare as an extension of warfare in Europe. The attitude that 'any good soldier should be able to handle guerrillas' betrayed the belief that insurgency was merely a technical problem. An overwhelming application of firepower or some technology that guaranteed mobility was the solution. Belloc might be updated to read, 'Whatever happens, we have got/The helicopter and they have not.' The temptation was to operationalize strategy, rather than treat insurgency, as did Wellesley, as a political problem which required the correct mix of politics and force. In any case, those nations, like France or Holland, who insisted on fighting to restore the imperial status quo in Indo-China, Algeria or Indonesia, were destined to fail.

In Vietnam, the United States assumed that politics and firepower were on their side. Unfortunately for Washington, the Communists were seen as the legitimate heirs of the anti-colonial revolution, while technology could never be more than a secondary factor in determining the success or failure of imperial campaigns.

That said, T. E. Lawrence's prediction of the guerrilla's inevitable victory was also optimistic. The transfer of nationalism and Marxism to the colonies did no more than make the playing field more level. Modern insurgencies are civil wars as much as were their imperial antecedents. A successful insurgency requires a collective sense of grievance to unite a critical mass of supporters behind a common cause. Tribal, religious and ethnic divisions work to divide that response, isolate the insurgents, and forfeit the moral high ground in the modern era as much as they did in the past. Possession of the mandate of heaven – that is, legitimacy – is as important to victory in the twenty-first century as it was in the eighteenth. Nor do strategic principles change over time. The insurgent cause is greatly advanced if it has outside support. The victory of insurgencies in China, Vietnam and Algeria owed much to the actions of outside powers. Where insurgencies lacked outside support, as in the Philippines, Malaya and eventually Greece after the Second World War, they failed. Time continues to favour the side which knows how best to use it. In the past, protraction usually, although not invariably, worked to the advantage of the imperial invader, because the resistance lacked the organizational structure, social and political cohesion and the economic base to sustain prolonged campaigns. Even when the resistance generated a leader of genius able to turn attrition against the invaders – an Abd el-Kader, Shamil, Samori, or de Wet – indigenous societies seldom possessed the social and political cohesiveness to sustain that strategy, or make the invaders pay a price high enough to cause them to leave. There were exceptions to this, of course. The British abandoned North America, the French, Saint Domingue in 1804, Mexico in 1867, and the Spanish, South America and Cuba in 1898. But overall, indigenous societies lacked an adequate base of operations, or were too riven by tribal, ethnic, geographic, even class divisions to be able to come together for anything more than sporadic violence against the outsider. This may have changed somewhat in the modern world, when the invader may be tempted to walk away from a conflict whose cost is too high, merely because the value of the objective simply does not justify the expenditure of resources.

On a tactical level, the lessons of imperial warfare were surprisingly modern. While many of the peoples who confronted Western armies might possess superb skills as warriors, they lacked the discipline to devise tactical systems that would pay off in operational and strategic terms. The triumph of Western imperial armies cannot be explained mainly by a superiority in weaponry. On occasion, firepower might cause an indigenous resistance to pay a devastating price for tactical mistakes, one which might cause resistance to unravel. But even then, battlefield victory was seldom decisive – that is, it seldom decided the outcome of a war – because elements of the resistance would elect to fight on. Indigenous resistance might find ways to overcome Western superiority in firepower through the use of surprise and terrain. As in imperial warfare, technology applied in a counter-insurgency situation is not a war winner by itself. It is merely a facilitator which improves operational efficiency and might reduce the costs in lives to levels acceptable at home. Technology gives the incumbent power the capacity to achieve operational and tactical efficiency, and to sustain attrition strategies.

Successful modern insurgencies, like ancient ones, usually succeeded because of contingent circumstances. Japanese expansion in Asia before and during the Second World War allowed relatively weak Communist or nationalist movements in China, Indo-China and the Dutch East Indies to expand into a vacuum. Intelligence, surprise, mobility, and the ability to control the strategic pace of a war were as important in Westmoreland's Vietnam as in Wellesley's India. General Jacques Massu's use of *quadrillage* – that is, dividing the battlefield into manageable segments – in the 1957 battle of Algiers owed much to General Lazare Hoche's approach to the suppression of the Vendéan insurgency of 1796. What the French commanders in Algiers neglected to learn from their illustrious forebears was the importance of the political dimension of counter-insurgency. Callwell believed Hoche achieved success 'as much by his happy combination of clemency with firmness, as by his masterly dispositions in the theatre of war to ensure a lasting peace. The overawing and not the exasperation of the enemy is the end to be kept in view'. Sir Robert Templer's hearts-and-minds approach to the Malayan insurgency was no more than updated Hoche. Generals Joseph Gallieni and Hubert Lyautey operating in Tonkin, Madagascar and Morocco in the years before the First World War called it 'peaceful penetration' – using economic and political incentives to gain the loyalty of the population, reserving the force of arms for the hold-outs. Resettlement and strategic hamlet strategies used in Malaya, Algeria and Vietnam were simply the lineal descendants of the 'clear the fields and strengthen the walls' approach used by Chinese officials to defeat the Taiping and Nien rebellions. These Chinese officials also realized that the main purpose of the militia was to filter out and identify disloyal and heterodox elements, rather than to fight *per se*.

Australian soldiers, sent to restore order following violence in the wake of a pro-independence vote in East Timor, round up anti-independence militiamen near Dili in September 1999. Modern peacekeeping and peacemaking operations can be viewed as a revival of the imperial mission to reduce zones of instability.

The 'New World Order' pronounced by American President George Bush in the wake of the Cold War may be viewed as a revival of imperialism, a softer, gentler version shorn of its racist overtones, but imperialism none the less. That imperialism is enjoying a comeback is hardly surprising. Imperialism was imbedded in notions of the superiority of Western culture and values. The failure of many ex-colonies to create successful political and economic systems, together with the collapse of Soviet Communism, has revived the belief that the spread of democracy and market economies – 'engagement and

Ethnic Albanian refugees from Kosovo fill Dutch army vehicles to travel to camps in southern Albania in May 1999. Ethnic cleansing and genocide have joined a list of crimes against humanity that 'engagement and enlargement' is meant to curtail.

enlargement' in the parlance of the Clinton administration – is in everyone's interest. The military implications of this are that Western armies will increasingly intervene to end famine, arbitrate ethnic cleansing, and engage in nation building. Many modern soldiers decry peace operations, military operations other than war, or stability and support missions in places like Haiti, Somalia, Rwanda, Bosnia, Kosovo or East Timor as perversions of the military's true role, which is to fight and win its nation's wars. However, peace operations would strike men like Hoche, Gallieni, Lyautey, or Funston very much as business as usual, either as stand-alone or as part of counter-insurgency strategies. Peace operations are not so much part of a new world order, but the resurrection of the old world order which was temporarily suspended during the Cold War.

Glossary

EIGHTEENTH-CENTURY NEW WORLD

GEORGE WASHINGTON (1732–99)
Born Westmoreland County, Virginia, of a prosperous planter father. Washington saw service in the French and Indian Wars as commander of all Virginia forces from 1755 and aide-de-camp of General Edward Braddock. Elected to the First Continental Congress in 1774 and named commander-in-chief of the Continental Army in June 1775. He routed British forces at Trenton on Christmas Eve 1776, held his army together during the terrible winter at Valley Forge in 1777–8, and defeated Cornwallis at Yorktown in 1781, effectively ending the American Revolution.

LOUIS-JOSEPH DE MONTCALM-GROZON (1712–59)
Born in Condiac, France. He captured the British posts at Oswego and Fort William Henry during the French and Indian War, and successfully defended Ticonderoga against a British attack in 1758. Died defending Quebec against an amphibious attack by General Wolfe.

JAMES WOLFE (1727–59)
Born in Westerham, Kent. Commissioned in 1741, he campaigned against the Jacobites in Scotland in 1745–6, and participated in the second seizure of Louisbourg in 1758. Died at Quebec while commanding a daring and successful amphibious assault against the French citadel.

TOUSSAINT L'OUVERTURE (1746–1803)
Brilliant leader of the ex-slaves who revolted in Saint Domingue in the wake of the French Revolution. Toussaint successfully manoeuvred against Spanish, British, French planter and Creole armies until he was treacherously captured and sent to France, where he perished miserably in prison.

INDIA

JOSEPH-FRANÇOIS DUPLEIX (1697–1763)
Son of a director in the French East India Company, Dupleix was named governor-general of all French establishments in India in 1742. In 1746 he seized Madras, which was returned to Britain by the 1748 treaty ending the War of Austrian Succession. He continued to intrigue unsuccessfully against

his chief British rival Robert Clive to expand French influence in India. Having met only defeat and in the process exhausted French finances, he was recalled to Paris in 1754 and died discredited and in obscurity.

ROBERT CLIVE (1725–74)

Clive joined the East India Company in 1743 and took part in the battles to avenge the Black Hole of Calcutta, when a number of British died after being locked up in a small and airless prison by the nawab of Bengal on 20 June 1756. At Plassey in 1757, Clive defeated a large Indian–French force, and subsequently became *de facto* ruler of Bengal. He was lionized in England on his return in 1760, entered parliament and was elevated to the Irish peerage two years later. He returned to Calcutta in 1765 to put order into a company and an army regarded as inefficient and undisciplined. However, the rigour of his reforms made him many enemies and resulted in his recall to England in 1767 to appear before a committee of inquiry.

TIPU SULTAN (1749–99)

Sultan of Mysore who was a staunch opponent of British encroachment in India. In 1789, he invaded the British protectorate of Travancore, provoking a two year conflict during which he was defeated by Cornwallis. In 1799, he attempted to reverse this verdict and in the process recover lost territory, but was killed when his capital city Seringapatam fell to the British.

SIR CHARLES NAPIER (1782–1853)

A soldier who had seen service in Ireland during the rebellion, Portugal in 1810 and the United States in 1813, Napier participated in the final campaign against Napoleon in 1815. In 1841 he took command of British forces in the Sind and defeated the amirs at the battle of Miani in 1843. As this exceeded his orders, the satirical magazine *Punch* suggested that his victory announcement should read simply '*Peccavi*', Latin for 'I have sinned' (i.e. 'I have Sind').

SIR ARTHUR WELLESLEY, DUKE OF WELLINGTON (1769–1852)

Of Anglo-Irish background, Wellesley joined the army in 1787 and was sent to India with his regiment. Named Governor of Mysore in 1799, he participated in the siege of Seringapatam that resulted in the death of Tipu Sultan. Wellesley defeated the Marathas at the battle of Assaye in 1803, which, he insisted at the end of his distinguished career, was 'the bloodiest for the numbers that I ever saw,' and 'the best thing' he ever did in the way of fighting. He was knighted in 1804 and returned to England a major general in September 1805. He applied many of the tactical lessons that he had learned in India in his campaigns against the French in Spain.

SOUTH AMERICA

SIMON BOLÍVAR (1783–1830)

Born in Caracas, Bolívar was proclaimed president of the Republic of Colombia (which included the modern states of Colombia, Venezuela and Ecuador) in 1819. After defeating the Spaniards in his home state in 1822, he took part in the final campaign in Peru in 1824. Although called 'The Liberator', Bolívar's rule was increasingly contested and he was forced to resign and go into exile in 1830.

JOSÉ DE SAN MARTÍN (1778–1850)

A native of Argentina, San Martín led an army across the Andes into Chile in 1817 where he defeated the Spanish at Chacubuco, and again the following year at Maipó. He captured Lima and was proclaimed Protector of Peru in 1821. He resigned after disagreements with Bolívar and finished his life in exile in France.

ALGERIA

THOMAS-ROBERT BUGEAUD (1784–1849)

Bugeaud served with Napoleonic armies in Spain, retiring after 1815 to farm, but returning to the army in 1830 on the fall of the Bourbon Restoration. Sent to Algeria in 1836, he defeated Abd el-Kader at the Sikkak river. An outspoken critic of Algerian colonization, he returned in 1841 to find the French army making many of the mistakes he had seen in the Peninsular War. He launched a campaign of attrition against the dissident Algerian tribes that led to the defeat of Abd el-Kader at Isly in 1844. He resigned as governor-general in 1847 after the French government failed to support his plans for military colonization. Commander in Paris in 1848, he unsuccessfully defended the July Monarchy against the revolution of that year.

ABD EL-KADER (1808–83)

As emir of Mascara, Abd el-Kader gradually consolidated his power in Oran province from 1832, occupied Miliana and Médéa and routed the

French at the Macta Marshes in 1835. Although defeated by Bugeaud at the Sikkak river in 1836, he skilfully convinced the general to sign the Treaty of Tafna that actually increased the territory under his control. By 1838, using a core regular army of 2,000 men supported by tribal levies, Abd el-Kader had extended his realm from the Moroccan frontier to the Kabylia. The emir's attack against French settlers on the Mitidja Plain in 1840 touched off a bitter seven year war that witnessed the return of Bugeaud. The French general combined mobile columns with scorched earth tactics to keep the emir's forces both starving and on the run. Abd el-Kader's defeat at Isly in 1844 caused the Sultan of Morocco to withdraw his support for the Algerian resistance. The emir surrendered to the French in 1847, was interned in France and in 1852 exiled to Damascus where he lived out his life in some style on a generous French pension. In 1871, he disowned one of his sons who supported the Kabylia revolt against the French.

LOUIS-NAPOLEON BONAPARTE (1808–73)
Third son of Louis Bonaparte, King of Holland and brother of Napoleon I. Louis Napoleon grew up in exile after the Bonapartes were expelled from France in 1816. He returned in 1848 to be elected President of the Second Republic and, from 1852, Emperor of the French. His early desire to abandon Algeria came to nothing. Encouraged by his Spanish-born empress Eugénie, he unwisely committed French troops to Mexico in 1862. After the Franco-Prussian War, he went into exile in England. His son, the Prince Impérial, was killed by the Zulus while serving in the British Army.

CAUCASUS

SHAMIL (1797?–1871)
In 1834, Shamil became leader of the Muridis, a Sufi (mystical Islamic) brotherhood that had declared a holy war when the Russians seized Dagestan in 1813. He declared Dagestan an independent state and led a series of raids on Russian positions in the Caucasus. An 1838 Russian expedition failed to capture Shamil, although it seized his capital at Ahulgo. Following the end of the Crimean War, with aid to Shamil from Turkey and Britain severed, the Russians launched an ambitious multi-pronged offensive against his mountain stronghold. His followers exhausted, his citadel at Vedeno taken in April 1859, Shamil surrendered to the Russians in September of that year. He was exiled to Kaluga, south of Moscow and allowed to make a pilgrimage to Mecca in 1870.

CHINA

LIN TSE-HSU (1785–1850)

Son of a poor teacher, Lin passed the highest level of the Chinese civil service examinations in 1811, after which he joined the Hanlin Academy, the body that advised the emperor. He subsequently held some of the most senior administrative posts in the empire during which time he earned the nickname 'Lin the Clear Sky'. In 1838, Lin was appointed imperial commissioner with extraordinary powers to deal with opium smuggling. When the British initiated the first Opium War after Lin destroyed large stocks of opium in Canton, the emperor reluctantly retired him. Lin was subsequently recalled to suppress Muslim rebels in Yunnan. He died on his way to deal with the Taiping rebellion. Lin is viewed as a national hero in China because of his stance against the British and as a precursor of the 'Self-Strengthening Movement'.

CHARLES 'CHINESE' GORDON (1833–85)

Trained at the Woolwich Academy, Gordon joined the Royal Engineers in 1852. A veteran of the Crimean War, he went to China where he participated in local army reform and fought against the Taiping rebellion, in the process earning his nickname. In 1877, he was appointed Governor of the Sudan, although he resigned that post in 1880. In 1884, he returned to extract the garrison at Khartoum, was besieged for ten months, and perished in 1885 when the Mahdi's troops stormed the city.

UNITED STATES

OSCEOLA (1804–38)

Born in Georgia, Osceola, also known as Powell, began to organize opposition in 1832 against efforts to remove the Seminoles from Florida. In 1835, he murdered a chief preparing to emigrate to Oklahoma with his people as well as a general sent to organize the departure, thereby touching off the Second Seminole War. For the next two years, he successfully resisted the troops sent against him using guerrilla tactics and ambushes. In 1837, he was seized at St Augustine while under a flag of truce and moved to Fort Moultrie at Charleston, SC, where he died. The war continued sporadically until 1842.

SITTING BULL (TATANKA YOTANKA) (1831?–90)

Born in present-day South Dakota, his reputation as a warrior and shaman caused him to become a chief of the Northern Sioux by 1866. The 1868 peace that he signed with the US government broke down from 1874 after gold was discovered in the Black Hills. He formed an alliance with the Arapaho and Cheyenne that culminated in the defeat of Custer at the Little Bighorn in 1876, although he was not present at the battle. He led his people into Canada to escape retribution, but was forced back into the United States in 1881 and was arrested. After serving a two-year imprisonment, he joined Buffalo Bill's Wild West Show. He was arrested for supporting the Ghost Dance movement and shot by an Amerindian policeman.

GEORGE ARMSTRONG CUSTER (1839–76)

Graduated last in his West Point class of 1861, Custer nevertheless staked out a brilliant career as a cavalry commander in the American Civil War, from which he emerged in 1865 as a 23-year-old brigadier general. Reduced to the rank of captain at the war's end, he established a reputation as an intrepid, if incautious and egotistical, Amerindian fighter, as well as an opponent of corruption in the Indian Bureau. While participating in the campaign to force the Cheyenne and Sioux on to reservations, he came upon a large encampment along the Little Bighorn river in the Montana territory on 25 June 1876. Believing the Indians were about to flee, he divided his force and set off in pursuit. Instead, the Indians turned on Custer, annihilating him and over two hundred of his men.

GERONIMO (GOYATHLAY) (1829–1909)

Chiricahua Apache war chief born in present-day Arizona, Geronimo was engaged in fighting the encroachment of settlers from Mexico or the United States from an early age. Although confined to reservations, he constantly escaped and continued to raid, often out of Mexico. A campaign launched against Geronimo in 1885 required 5,000 troops and eighteen months to track him and thirty-five of his followers down. Confined to Florida, he was eventually allowed to settle on a reservation in Oklahoma, where he became a successful farmer and converted to Christianity. He rode in President Theodore Roosevelt's inaugural parade in 1905 and published his autobiography the following year.

GEORGE CROOK (1829–1890)

An 1852 graduate of West Point, Crook led a Union brigade at Antietam in 1862 and campaigned in the Shenandoah Valley under Sheridan in 1864. As an Amerindian fighter, he successfully pacified the Apaches under Cochise (1871–3), but was defeated by Crazy Horse at Rosebud Creek in 1876. His troops pursued the Sioux for almost a year after the Little Bighorn in an operation that became a severe test of endurance. He campaigned against Geronimo in Arizona in 1882 and 1883. Despite his reputation as an Amerindian fighter, Crook was a strong advocate of Amerindian rights.

NELSON A. MILES (1839–1925)
Commissioned in the 22nd Massachusetts at the outbreak of the Civil War, by 1865 Miles was a brigadier general with a Congressional Medal of Honor, having fought in almost every major campaign with the Army of the Potomac. He was Jefferson Davis' jailer at Fortress Monroe, Virginia. He fought against Chief Joseph (1877) and Geronimo in 1886. He was severely criticized for the massacre of Sioux at Wounded Knee in 1890. He became commander-in-chief of the US Army in 1895, and led the occupation of Puerto Rico in 1898, retiring from the army in 1903.

ALFRED THAYER MAHAN (1840–1914)
Son of the celebrated professor of tactics at West Point, Dennis Hart Mahan, Alfred Thayer served in the US Navy during the American Civil War, eventually rising to become president of the Naval War College in Newport, RI. He achieved international prominence with the 1890 publication of *The Influence of Sea Power upon History*, which argued that England's economic prosperity was built on the foundation of a large navy. By extension, Mahan's argument assumed the need for colonial naval bases to support an extensive trade network. He became president of the American Historical Association in 1902 and retired in 1906 a rear admiral.

FREDERICK FUNSTON (1865–1914)
Son of an Ohio congressman, Funston volunteered to serve with the Cubans to fight the Spaniards in 1896. When the Spanish American War broke out he joined the US Army in the Philippines, and was promoted to brigadier general. He crafted the strategy to defeat the Philippine insurgents, culminating in the daring raid that captured Aguinaldo in March 1901. In 1914, he commanded US forces that seized Vera Cruz during the unrest in Mexico.

EMILIO AGUINALDO (1869–1964)
Of Chinese and Tagalog parentage, he was active in local politics and leader of a revolutionary society. In 1897, he departed the Philippines in return for

a promise of significant reforms from the Spanish governor. However, encouraged by the Americans, he returned to the Philippines to become president of the provisional government proclaimed on 12 June 1898. When the Philippines were ceded to the United States by the Treaty of Paris in December 1898, Aguinaldo's relations with the Americans deteriorated. When hostilities broke out in Manila on 4 February 1899, Aguinaldo declared war on the United States. The war raged for three years until General Frederick Funston captured Aguinaldo in his secret headquarters at Palanan in Northern Luzon in March 1901. Aguinaldo took an oath of allegiance and was granted a pension from the American government. He was defeated when he ran for president of the Philippines in 1935. The Americans again arrested him for collaboration with the occupying Japanese in 1945, but he was subsequently amnestied.

AFRICA

LOUIS FAIDHERBE (1818–89)
Appointed Governor of Senegal in 1854, Faidherbe began the expansion that transformed Senegal from a coastal base to a colony with a substantial hinterland. In the process he is given credit for creating the *tirailleurs sénégalais*. An unsuccessful general in the Franco-Prussian War of 1870–71, he wrote pioneering studies on the anthropology of Algiers and the French Sudan and of the Fula and Berber languages in the post-war years.

CHARLES MANGIN (1866–1925)
Mangin's family opted for French nationality when their hometown was absorbed into German annexed Lorraine at the conclusion of the Franco-Prussian War. Commissioned in the colonial infantry out of St Cyr in 1888, Mangin saw service in the Western Sudan and led the advanced guard of the Marchand mission that traversed Africa in 1896–8. After further tours in West Africa and Indo-China, Mangin came to Morocco where he captured Marrakesh in 1912. However, he quarrelled with Lyautey after his aggressive tactics and high casualties raised protests in France. Mangin's 1910 book *La force noire* passionately advocated the use of Black African troops to supplement French numerical inferiority *vis-à-vis* Germany. Mangin's First World War career was brilliant, if controversial, especially after his Sixth Army, badly blooded in Mangin's impetuous offensives, became a centre of the 1917 mutinies. He was relieved by Clemenceau in 1919 for promoting the Rhenish separatist movement in occupied Germany.

JOSEPH GALLIENI (1849–1916)

Gallieni graduated from St Cyr into the Franco-Prussian War, where he participated in the heroic defence by French marines of Bazailles near Sedan, was wounded and made a POW. He served in West Africa from 1876. In Tonkin from 1893, he pioneered the 'oil spot' methods which he saw as the antidote to the destructive methods of colonial conquest he had witnessed in Africa. Resident general of Madagascar between 1896 and 1905, he returned to France as an immensely respected soldier. He rejected the post of commander-in-chief in 1911, and instead recommended Joseph Joffre, who had once been his subordinate in the colonies. Many credit Gallieni with prodding Joffre to take advantage of German over-extension on the Marne in 1914, and for pioneering mechanized infantry when he requisitioned Paris taxis and buses to ferry troops to the front lines. Named war minister in 1915, Gallieni attempted without success to remove Joffre. He died on the operating table in May 1916, after denouncing Joffre's failures at Verdun. He was posthumously named Marshal of France in 1921.

HUBERT LYAUTEY (1854–1934)

A cavalryman of aristocratic background and royalist opinions, Lyautey's commitment to Social Catholicism caused him in 1890 to publish a controversial article in the prestigious *Revue des Deux Mondes* criticizing officers for, among other things, caring more about their horses than their men. This, together with other non-traditional aspects of Lyautey's lifestyle including his alleged homosexuality, caused him to be assigned to Tonkin, where he became an enthusiastic promoter of Gallieni's 'oil spot' methods of 'peaceful penetration.' He followed Gallieni to Madagascar where he took responsibility for the pacification of the southern half of the island. In 1903, at the special request of the governor-general, he was called to southeastern Algeria to deal with raiders out of Morocco. Lyautey's solution was to create mobile flying columns *à la Bugeaud*, and to seize forward bases inside territory claimed, but not controlled, by the Sultan of Morocco. Recalled to France in 1910 to command an army corps, he returned to Morocco as the first resident general from 1912. He served briefly as war minister (1916-17), was promoted Marshal of France in 1921, but retired in 1925 over criticism of his handling of the Rif War.

JULES FERRY (1832–1893)

Best known for his 1882 law which resulted in the creation of the French system of free, secular and compulsory education, Ferry was also an enthusiastic proponent of imperial expansion. As prime minister, he promoted France's seizure of Tunisia (1881), the campaign to take over Tonkin and Annam (1883–5), the French Congo (1884–5), and an unsuccessful bid for Madagascar (1885). However, the French setback at Lang Son on the Chinese border in 1885 brought down his ministry. Elected to the Senate, he continued to be at the centre of controversy and was assassinated in 1893.

SAMORI TOURÉ (1830–1900)

Samori abandoned trade to become a warrior in 1851, eventually establishing an empire on the right bank of the Niger. He used Islam to insure the cohesion of his empire. But its fundamental strength lay in the efficiency of his military organization that combined a corps of élite *sofas* or warriors with a militia raised from the provinces of his empire. His armies were well disciplined, made excellent use of cavalry, and were expert at laying ambushes. Samori financed arms purchases by taxes paid in agricultural products, the gold fields of Buré, and by slave trading. The French campaigned against him in 1881 and 1885. Gallieni provoked a rebellion in part of his empire in 1888–90. A French offensive in 1891 forced him to move to the area that includes the north of the Ivory Coast and part of Ghana. Captured in August 1898, Samori was exiled to Gabon.

BOER WAR

FREDERICK SLEIGH ROBERTS (1832–1914)

Born in Cawnpore, India, and trained at Sandhurst, Roberts won a Victoria Cross during the Indian Mutiny. On 1 September 1880, he defeated Ayub Khan near Kandahar in Afghanistan. He served as commander-in-chief in India between 1885 and 1893, and was named field marshal in 1895. He served as supreme commander during the Boer War between December 1899 and November 1900, relieving Kimberley. He was made an earl in 1901.

HERBERT KITCHENER (1850–1916)

Of Anglo-Irish descent, Kitchener joined the Royal Engineers in 1871, serving in Palestine, Cyprus and the Sudan. He defeated the Mahdi's forces at Omdurman in 1898, negotiated Marchand's departure from Fashoda, and became successfully Chief of Staff and commander-in-chief in South Africa during the Boer War. Made a viscount, he became commander-in-chief in India (1902–9) and consul-general in Egypt (1911). As secretary for war in 1914, he organized the New Armies. He was lost when the HMS *Hampshire* hit a mine off Orkney in 1916.

REDVERS BULLER (1839–1908)
A veteran of service in China (1860), the Red River Expedition (1870), the Ashanti War (1874), the Kaffir War (1878) and the Zulu War (1879) during which he won the VC. He served as Chief of Staff in the First South African War (1881) and briefly as commander-in-chief during the Second South African War (1899–1900), during which he raised the siege of Ladysmith.

CECIL RHODES (1853–1902)
Originally sent to South Africa for his health, he made a huge fortune in the diamond diggings of Kimberley, where he amalgamated several companies to form the De Beers firm in 1888. He returned to England to study at Oxford. Elected to the Cape House of Assembly, he secured Bechuanaland as a protectorate (1884) and a charter for the British South Africa Company (1889), whose land was later named Rhodesia. He became prime minister of the Cape Colony, but was forced to resign in 1896 following the Jameson Raid. He organized the defences of Kimberley during the Second South African War.

JAN CHRISTIAAN SMUTS (1870–1950)
Born in the Cape Colony, he studied at Cambridge and became a lawyer. At the outbreak of the Second South African War he joined the Boers and served as a guerrilla leader. After the war he entered the House of Assembly, held several cabinet posts, led campaigns against the Germans in South West Africa and Tanganyika, and succeeded Botha as premier. He played a prominent role in the founding of the League of Nations, helped to found the United Party in 1934, and became Prime Minister of South Africa in 1939.

CHRISTIAAN DE WET (1854–1922)
De Wet fought in the First South African War and commanded the Orange Free State forces in 1899. He became the most audacious of the Boer commanders in the Second South African War. After the war, he was increasingly at odds with Botha's policy of reconciliation with the British. In 1914, he joined the Afrikaner insurrection which broke out when Botha organized an invasion of German South West Africa. De Wet was captured and sentenced to six years' imprisonment. He was released the following year and returned to his farm.

LOUIS BOTHA (1862–1919)
A politician who in the 1890s had opposed President Kruger's hostile policy toward the British, Botha commanded the Boer forces besieging Ladysmith

at the beginning of the war. He succeeded Joubert as commander-in-chief in March 1900. After the fall of Pretoria, Botha helped to organize the guerrilla campaign. He was one of the signatories to the Peace of Vereeniging that ended the war in May 1902. In 1907, he became prime minister of the Transvaal colony, and in 1910 the first premier of the Union of South Africa.

RUSSO-JAPANESE WAR

SERGEI WITTE (1849–1915)

Following graduation from university in Odessa, Witte joined the railway administration. He first came to prominence during the Russo-Turkish War (1877–8) for his innovative organization of supply to the front. In subsequent years, he impressed his superiors with his theories and statistical approach to the use of railways for economic development. In 1889, Witte joined the ministry of finance and rose to be its head in 1892. There, he raised huge loans abroad to finance Russian industrial development and to complete the Trans-Siberian Railway begun in 1891. He was removed from office in 1903, but returned in 1905 to negotiate the peace with Japan, and to become prime minister. However, he was forced to resign in 1906 following the wake of unrest caused by defeat in that war. In 1914, he unsuccessfully opposed the entry of Russia into the First World War.

KOSHAKU TOGO HEIHACHIRO (1848–1934)

Togo studied naval science in England between 1871 and 1878. In December 1903 he became commander-in-chief of the combined fleet and was made admiral in 1904. Togo directed the naval blockade of Port Arthur that ended in its surrender on 2 January 1905. On 27 May he destroyed 33 out of the 35 Russian ships that appeared in the Tsushima Strait. His manoeuvre to cross the Russian T on two occasions during the battle became a standard study in naval staff schools. Togo subsequently became chief of the Naval General Staff and war counsellor to the emperor. In 1913 he became fleet admiral, and was placed in charge of the education of Hirohito.

Further Reading

Allen, W. E. D. and Muratoff, Paul, *Caucasian Battlefields. A History of the Wars on the Turco-Caucasian Border 1828–1921* (Cambridge University Press, Cambridge, England, 1953)

Baumann, Robert F., 'Russian-Soviet Unconventional Wars in the Caucasus, Central Asia and Afghanistan', *Leavenworth Papers no. 20* (Combat Studies Institute, Fort Leavenworth, KS, 1993)

Bond, Brian, *Victorian Military Campaigns* (Praeger, New York, 1967)

Bowle, John, *The Imperial Achievement* (Little Brown, Boston, 1973)

Broxup, Marie Benningsen (ed.), *The North Caucasus Barrier. The Russian Advance towards the Muslim World* (St Martin's Press, New York, 1992)

Callwell, Colonel C. E., *Small Wars. Their Principles and Practice* (Bison Books, Lincoln, NE, 1996)

Clayton, Anthony, *France, Soldiers and Africa* (Brassey's, New York and London, 1988)

Demelas, M.-D and Saint-Geours, Y., *La vie quotidienne en Amerique du Sud au temps de Bolivar 1809–1830* (Hachette, Paris, 1987)

Drechsler, Horst, *Let Us Die Fighting* (Zed Press, London, 1980)

Eccles, W. J., *France in America* (Michigan State University Press, East Lansing, MI, 1990)

Evans-Prichard, *The Sanusi of Cyrenaica* (Oxford University Press, Oxford, 1954)

Fieldhouse, D. K., *The Colonial Empires* (London, 1966)

Fuller, William, *Strategy and Policy in Russia 1600–1914* (Free Press, New York, 1992)

Geyer, Dietrich, *Russian Imperialism. The Iteration of Domestic and Foreign Policy, 1860–1914* (Yale University Press, New Haven, Conn, 1987)

Gollwitzer, Heinz, *Europe in the Age of Imperialism, 1880–1914* (New York, 1969)

Greene, Jerome A., *Yellowstone Command. Colonel Nelson A. Miles and the Great Sioux War 1876–1877* (University of Nebraska Press, Lincoln, NE, 1991)

Gump, James O., *The Dust Rose Like Smoke. The Subjugation of the Zulu and the Sioux* (University of Nebraska Press, Lincoln, NE, 1994)

Harries, Meirion and Susie, *Soldiers of the Sun. The Rise and Fall of the Imperial Japanese Army* (Random House, New York, 1992)

Hunczak, Taras, *Russian Imperialism from Ivan the Great to the Revolution* (Rutgers University Press, New Jersey, 1974)

Ion, A. Hamish and Errington, E. J., *Great Powers and Little Wars. The Limits of Power* (Praeger, Westport, Conn. and London, 1993)

Jansen, Marius B., *The Cambridge History of Japan*, vol. 5, *The Nineteenth Century* (Cambridge University Press, Cambridge, England, 1993)

Julien, Charles-Andree, *Histoire de l'Algerie Contemporaine,* vol. I, *Conquite et Colonisation* (Presses Universitaire de France, Paris, 1964).

Khalfin, N. A., *Russia's Policy in Central Asia 1857–1868* (London, 1964)

Kanya-Forstner, A. S., *The Conquest of the Western Sudan. A Study in French Military Imperialism* (Cambridge University Press, Cambridge, England, 1969)

Kuhn, Philip A., *Rebellion and its Enemies in Late Imperial China. Militarization and Social Structure, 1796–1864* (Harvard University Press, Cambridge, MA, 1970)

LaFeber, Walter, *The New Empire. An Interpretation of American Expansion 1860–1898* (Cornell University Press, Ithaca, NY, 1971)

Lowie, Robert H., *Indians of the Plains (University of Nebraska Press, Lincoln, NE, 1982)*

Mackesy, Piers, *The War for America 1775–1783* (University of Nebraska Press, Lincoln, NE, 1992)

Mahon, John K., *History of the Second Seminole War, 1835–1842* (University of Florida Press, Gainesville, FL, 1967)

Malone, Patrick M., *The Skulking Way of War. Technology and Tactics among the New England Indians* (Johns Hopkins University Press, Baltimore and London, 1993)

Morris, James, *Heaven's Command. An Imperial Progress* (Harvest Books, New York and London, 1973)

Pakenham, Thomas, *The Boer War* (Weidenfeld and Nicolson, London, 1979)

Perez, Louis, *Cuba. Between Reform and Revolution* (Oxford University Press, New York and Oxford, 1988)

Porch, Douglas, *The Conquest of Morocco* (Knopf, New York, 1982 and Jonathan Cape, London, 1986)

Porch, Douglas, *The Conquest of the Sahara* (Knopf New York, 1984 and Jonathan Cape, London, 1984)

Porch, Douglas, *The French Foreign Legion* (Harper Collins, New York, 1991 and Macmillan, London, 1991)

Porch, Douglas, 'Bugeaud, Gallieni, Lyautey: The Development of French Colonial Warfare', in Peter Paret (ed.), *The Makers of Modern Strategy* (Princeton University Press, Princeton, N.J., 1986)

Porch, Douglas, 'Imperial Wars From the Seven Years War to the First World War', in Charles Townshend (ed.), *The Oxford Illustrated History of Modern War* (Oxford University Press, Oxford and New York, 1997)

Rediel, Carl W. (ed.), 'Transformation in Soviet and Russian Military History', *Proceedings of the Twelfth Military History Symposium, United States Air Force Academy, 1–3 October, 1986* (United States Air Force Academy, Office of Air Force History, Washington, DC, 1990)

Roberts, David, *Once They Moved Like the Wind. Cochise, Geronimo, and the Apache Wars* (Touchstone Books, New York, 1994)

Schweinitz, Karl de, *The Rise and Fall of British India* (Methuen, London and New York, 1983)

Smith, Woodruff D., *The German Colonial Empire* (University of North Carolina Press, Chapel Hill, NC, 1978)

Spear, Percival, *A History of India,* vol. 2 (Penguin Books, London, 1978)

Steele, Ian K., *Warpaths. Invasions of North America* (Oxford University Press, Oxford and New York, 1994)

Sullivan, Anthony Thrall, *Thomas-Robert Bugeaud, France and Algeria 1784–1849: Power, Politics and the Good Society* (Archon Books, Hamden, Conn., 1983)

Teng, S. Y., *The Nien Army and their Guerrilla Warfare, 1851–1868* (Mouton, The Hague, 1961)

Trask, David, *The War with Spain in 1898* (University of Nebraska Press, Lincoln, NE, 1981)

Twitchett, Denis and Fairbank, John K., *The Cambridge History of China,* vol. 10, *Late Ch'ing, 1800–1911* (Cambridge University Press, Cambridge, England, 1978)

Utley, Robert, *Frontier Regulars, The United States Army and the Indian 1866–1891* (New York, 1973)

Utley, Robert, *The Lance and the Shield. The Life and Times of Sitting Bull* (Henry Holt New York, 1993)

Warwick, Peter (ed.), *The South African War. The Anglo-Boer War 1899–1902* (Longmans, London, 1980)

Warner, Denis & Peggy, *The Tide at Sunrise. A History of the Russo-Japanese War of 1904–1905* (Charterhouse, New York, 1974)

Weller, Jac, *Wellington in India* (Longmans, London, 1972)

Westwood, J. N., *Russia Against Japan, 1904–05 A New Look at the Russo-Japanese War* (Macmillan, Basingstoke, 1986)

Index